PRINCIPLED POSITIONS
Postmodernism and the Rediscovery of Value

Principled Positions

Postmodernism and the Rediscovery of Value

edited by Judith Squires

LAWRENCE & WISHART
LONDON

Lawrence & Wishart Limited
144a Old South Lambeth Road
London SW8 1XX

First published in Great Britain 1993

© Lawrence & Wishart Limited

Each essay © the author, 1993

Cover design: Jan Brown Designs
Cover photo: Abel Lagos
Photoset in North Wales by
Derek Doyle & Associates, Mold, Clwyd.
Printed and bound in Great Britain by
Cambridge University Press.

For Linda Brandon (1960–1992)

Contents

Acknowledgements

This collection developed out of a conference entitled 'A Question of Value' which was held at the Institute of Contemporary Arts in December 1990. This was the last event I organised with Linda Brandon. I would like to thank the ICA staff for their help in realising this event, and also Bill McAlister, Erica Carter, Martha Russell, Donna Soto-Morettini and Jon Zeppetelli, for their support during the many preceding conferences and talks. I would also like to thank Matt Seaton, Sally Davison, Lindsay Thomas and Ruth Borthwick of Lawrence & Wishart for all their hard work in producing this volume. Thanks too to Ann, Barry, Dawn and Kate for their invaluable support.

Though most of the essays in this volume were written for the 'Question of Value' Conference, some have been published previously. I gratefully acknowledge the following previous publishers: Steven Connor, 'The Necessity of Value', in *Theory and Cultural Value*, Blackwell 1992. Paul Hirst, 'An Answer to Relativism?' in *New Formations* number 10 Spring 1990; Iris Marion Young, 'Together in Difference: Transforming the Logic of Group Political Conflict', in *Political Theory Newsletter* vol. 4 1992 pp.11–26; Christopher Norris 'Old Themes for New Times: Postmodernism, Theory and Cultural Politics', in *New Formations* number 18 Winter 1992.

Notes on Contributors

Steven Connor is Reader in Modern English Literature and Director of the Centre for Interdisciplinary Research in Culture and the Humanities at Birkbeck College, University of London. His most recent publications are *Postmodernist Culture: An Introduction to Theories of the Contemporary* (Blackwell) and *Theory and Cultural Value* (Blackwell).

David Harvey is the Halford Mackinder Professor of Geography at Oxford University. His books include *Social Justice and the City* (Blackwell), *The Urban Experience* (Blackwell) and *The Condition of Postmodernity* (Blackwell).

Paul Hirst is Professor of Social Theory at Birkbeck College, University of London. His most recent books are *After Thatcher* (Collins), *The pluralist Theory of the State: Selected Writings of G.D.H. Cole, J.N. Figgis and H.J. Laski* (Routledge), *Representative Democracy and Its Limits* (Polity) and *Associative Democracy* (Polity).

Chantal Mouffe is Programme Director at the College International de Philosophie, Paris. She is co-author, with Ernesto Laclau, of *Hegemony and Socialist Strategy* (Verso) and editor of *Dimensions of Radical Democracy* (Verso).

Christopher Norris is Professor of English at University College Cardiff. His books include: *The Deconstructive Turn* (1983), *Jacques Derrida* (1987), *What's Wrong With Postmodernism?* (1990) and *Uncritical Theory* (Lawrence & Wishart, 1992).

Kate Soper is Senior Lecturer in Philosophy at the University of North London. She is the author of *On Human Needs* (Harvester), *Humanism and Anti-Humanism* (Hutchinson) and *Troubled Pleasures* (Verso).

Judith Squires is a lecturer in Politics at Bristol University. She is editor of the journal *New Formations* and co-editor (with James Donald and Erica Carter) of *Space and Place: Theories of Identity and Location* (Lawrence & Wishart, 1993).

Jeffrey Weeks is Professor of Social Relations at the University of the West of England, Bristol. His most recent book is *Against Nature: Essays on history, sexuality and identity* (Rivers Oram Press, 1991) and he is currently working on a book on 'sexual values'.

Iris Marion Young is Professor of Public and International Affairs at the University of Pittsburgh, USA. She is author of *Justice and the Politics of Difference* (Princeton University Press) and *Throwing Like a Girl and other essays in Feminist Philosophy and Social Theory* (Indiana University Press).

Introduction

Postmodernism, in its infinitely skeptical and subversive attitude toward normative claims, institutional justice and political struggles, is certainly refreshing. Yet, it is also debilitating.

Seyla Benhabib[1]

The radical post-structuralist revolt against sameness has set the tone of recent debates. But the effect has been to throw out the living baby of political and ethical solidarities and similarities across differences, with the cold bathwater of capitalist imposed conceptions of universality and sameness.

David Harvey[2]

... as it is presently articulated, postmodernism inhibits the development of alternative concepts and practice of justice. This is so partially because many theorists do not pay adequate attention to the concrete workings of contemporary forms of domination.

Jane Flax[3]

The premise of this book is that although liberating, and even democratising, in its refusal of hierarchy and certainty, the postmodern condition is paralysing in its deconstruction of all 'principled positions'. The various contributors to the collection together present a discernible shift towards a reassertion of value, and an examination of the implications and effects of this shift within the political arena. The concern is to make this shift without relinquishing the critical gains made possible by the postmodern assertion of the need to respond contextually and strategically to shifting frameworks of

1

power and resistance, and to articulate a fuller recognition of multiplicity and difference. I have brought these pieces together by way of articulating, in the words of Kate Soper: 'a need for a post-post-structuralist programme in which we acknowledge more openly the latent metaphysical dependencies of the critical attempt to suppress value, without giving up on the gains which that critical move has brought us.'[4] A post-Enlightenment defence of principled positions, without the essentialist or transcendental illusions of Enlightenment thought, is both possible and necessary.

The contributors to this collection engage with both the theoretical and methodological implications of postmodernism and the moral and political aims of democratic pluralism. It is the attempt to negotiate the apparent contradictions between the two which unifies these essays. The contradictions are manifest at various levels of abstraction: from the epistemological issue of relativism and absolutism, particularism and universalism, through the moral issues of standards of judgments and evaluation, to the practical issues of political organisation, the mechanisms of representation and participation.

The postmodern condition may be characterised, following Jane Flax, as involving three key features: the death of Man, History and Metaphysics.[5] This involves the rejection of all essentialist and transcendental conceptions of human nature; the rejection of unity, homogeneity, totality, closure and identity; the rejection of the pursuit of the real and the true. In the place of these illusory ideals we find the assertion that man is a social, historical or linguistic artifact; the celebration of fragmentation, particularity and difference; the acceptance of the contingent and apparent.

Such a postmodern celebration of relativism and rejection of absolutism (or particularism over universalism) has led, as Soper notes, to a relativism of the vocabulary of 'judgement', 'worth' and 'merit' in aesthetics; 'rights', 'freedom' and 'duty' in ethics; and 'truth', 'verification' and 'objectivity' in epistemology; all are seen as discourse dependent. There is, we are often told, nothing outside the text. If this is accepted, it would appear that there remains no grounds for talk of transcendent values and no basis more solid than discursive agreement for the development of principled positions which might inform political action.

Such assumptions have become increasingly dominant within many forms of western intellectual discourse. Commitments to theoretical justifications of emancipatory projects have been largely submerged by what Norris characterises as an unfortunate 'proneness to the vagaries of Franco-phile intellectual fashion'; a symptom of our present malaise rather than a cure of modernism and its discontents.[6] Soper interprets such acceptance of the loss of values as a way of adjusting to the ugliness of our times; but an acceptance only available to those able to retreat into the playful world of postmodern cynicism. This loss of hope, of utopian vision, must then be a parochial privileged experience.[7] For talk of loss implies that there was a period of stability, groundedness, certainty. And this was never a reality for most. As Stuart Hall notes: 'Thinking about my own sense of identity, I realise that it has always depended on the fact of being a migrant, on the difference from the rest of you. So one of the fascinating things about this discussion is to find myself centred at last. Now that, in the postmodern age, you all feel so dispersed, I become centred.'[8]

To engage in more than theory, to recognise the position from which our theorising is possible, to acknowledge the motive for theorising at all, is to accept the existence of certain structures of oppression. For most of those who currently engage in a deconstruction of the claimed purity of theorising do so in the name of marginalised or oppressed groups.

We should, of course, note the distinction between the many forms of postmodernism and between deconstruction and postmodernism. Some manifestations of these are more open to the charges of moral and political debilitation than others. It has been stressed by some theorists that there are 'strong' and 'weak' (or 'soft sceptical') forms of postmodernism and that only the strong form undermines the possibility of normative criticism generally.[9] The strong form holds that the subject is merely another position in language. It rejects any historical narrative that focuses on the macro rather than micro and condemns all of western metaphysics for an imputed grounding of Truth in the Real. The weak form, on the other hand, posits an embedded rather than a purely fictive subject. It also involves the rejection, not of all macro-narratives, but of essentialist and monocausal grand-narratives. Finally, it involves the assertion of philosophy as the investigation of empirical conditions under which communities of interpretation generate validity claims. The strong form could be said to deny the possibility not only of meta-narratives of legitimation, but of the practice of context-transcending legitimation altogether.[10]

Others, most prominently Christopher Norris, distinguish between postmodernism and deconstruction and claim that the latter, but not the former, is compatible with grounded value commitments and avoids nominalism. For it is argued that deconstruction is a method for exposing the contradictions and assumptions within existing discourses. Or, as Gayatri Spivak has noted, deconstruction is 'more a way of looking than a programme for doing'.[11] Derridean deconstruction 'can lend itself neither to this politics, nor to that, neither to value commitments nor to their disowning.[12] It is therefore important to recognise the limits of deconstruction and not expect it to do all our work. What we do with this method will be dependent on values derived independently; upon our 'invented moralities'. 'I have,' says Spivak, 'very little patience with people who are so deeply into deconstruction and they have nothing else substantive to think about.'[13] It is not then that deconstruction itself denies the possibility of developing, articulating and acting upon principled positions, it is rather that many have assumed, I think wrongly, that it denied their credibility. Yet there are still all too many substantive things to think about. When faced with famime, war, poverty and oppression we need not forsake a morally grounded response and simply engage in ironic discursive games. The critical response to Baudrillard's assertions about the Gulf War, and Harvey's expressed concern at the lack of political reaction to the deaths of American workers, are just two manifestations of the growing concern about the practical implications of taking such a position.[14]

It is precisely such dangers which mobilise concern at the extent to which questions of meaning and interpretation have superseded questions of judgement and value. Steven Connor acknowledges this, yet also argues that the motivating impulse behind these interpretative strategies is often to be found in a desire to challenge the operation of marginalisation, domination and exclusion. Thus it is not that issues of values are absent, but that they are present 'sceptically, embarrassedly or partially'.[15] This reluctance to speak of the question of value within postmodern theories is simply problematic; values have not disappeared, but have been driven into the critical unconscious – continuing to exercise force but without being available for scrutiny. Indeed, Connor claims that despite the overt rejection of criteria for evaluation in recent times, there has been an intensification rather than a waning of ethical and evaluative concerns.

In this context, out of this impasse, Jeffrey Weeks calls for a move from tearing apart the pre-suppositions of western thought, to beginning the arduous task of re-thinking – the 'hard road to renewal'. The rejection of absolutism and essentialism, and an acceptance of relativism, need not lead to moral paralysis. It is only if we insist on adopting a strong form of postmodernism, or constructing an absolute opposition between objectivism and relativism, claiming that anything goes and avoiding all principled positions, that we undermine the possibility of sustaining the conditions for a tolerant and pluralistic intellectual and political order.

Avoiding this dualism, the contributors to this collection share, from admittedly distinct perspectives, a common concern to accept and retain some of the gains made by the critical mores of postmodernism, but also to recognise and surpass the problems involved in these attempts to suppress value. A synthetic approach is called for: Soper argues for giving up on the idea of a grand narrative of single truth without giving up on the idea of truth as a regulative ideal; Connor argues that the critique of the notion of value is not a denial of the possibility of evaluation in general, but a rejection of the unjustly limiting forms which aesthetic evaluation has taken; Hirst argues that there are many forms of relativism and not all involve the abandonment of the search for specific standards of validity; and Chantal Mouffe states that:

> What is at stake here is not a rejection of universalism in favour of particularism, but the need for a new type of articulation between the universal and the particular.[16]

Or, in the words of Jeffrey Weeks:

> The key issue is whether it is possible to find a common normative standard by which we can come to terms with different ways of life, whether we can balance relativism with some sense of minimum universal values.[17]

Thus we find a clear articulation within all of these pieces of one of the key dilemmas of contemporary theorising: how to balance a theoretical rejection of essentialism, objectivism and universalism with a moral and political commitment to non-oppressive, democratic and pluralistic values. How to locate a kind of politics which could embrace partial, contradictory, permanently unclosed constructions of personal and collective selves and still be faithful to the humanist politics of various emancipatory projects. How are we to assess the validity of these value claims? If, as Weeks asks, 'there is no foundation in nature, science or history for the truth claims of our belief systems, where, in our pluralistic universe, can truth or validity lie?'[18]

The most common response is to turn to inter-subjectively generated discursive agreements within specific communities or groups. If moralities, values and identities are not essential or absolute, if they are constructed and invented, then we must be concerned with the process of invention and articulation. This recognition is accompanied by a belief that our identities, values and moralities are constituted through communities. See, for example, Weeks: 'A community offers a "vocabulary of values" through which individuals construct their understanding of the social world, and of their sense of identity and belonging.'[19] Thus this path out of impasse asserts that rather than accepting a postmodern surrender to nihilism, we should look towards, and attempt to realise, communities in which there is the possibility of the development of a vocabulary of values in which all can share.

The extent to which these vocabularies are shared, the degree of inclusion and commonality, thus becomes crucial in the construction of ethical, aesthetic and epistemological criteria. These communities cannot be assumed to be homogeneous or hermetic. We must recognise that solidarity is often achieved at the expense of a two-fold strategy of exclusion and assimilation, a denial of difference. It is all too easy to construct ourselves through an assertion of sameness with particular others – a strategy which demands that we also assert our difference from those not within the community. In the terms of Iris Young, this 'logic of identity' requires exclusion of difference and therefore generates dichotomy not unity. In such circumstances narratives are delimited, identities are skewed and values partial along power-structured lines.

The 'logic of identity', or the 'absolutisation of difference' in Weeks' terms, is shown through deconstructive method, to produce categories which appear to be mutually exclusive, but in fact depend on one another. 'Deconstruction not only exposes the meaning of categories as contextual, but also reveals their differentiation from others as undecidable.'[20] The practical realities of social life defy the attempt to conceive and enforce group difference as exclusive opposition. To resolve differences in a democratic fashion, a more fluid, explicitly relational conception of difference is needed in order to recognise heterogeneity and interspersion of groups.

Young argues that 'social movements of oppressed or

disadvantaged groups need a political vision different from both the assimilationist and the separatist ideals.'[21] This political vision will require, minimally, that the groups in question understand themselves as participating in the same society. That is to say, a recognition of difference will also at the same time involve an assertion of some form of solidarity and agreement. This recognition is also present in the work of both Jeffrey Weeks and Chantal Mouffe. Both talk of the need to invent solidarities, to develop contingent communities based upon shared vocabularies of values: Weeks argues that we must embrace both solidarity and difference and Mouffe argues for a principle of democratic equivalence which does not eliminate difference.

Thus whilst Young uses deconstructive method to critique the logic of identity and to reject the political systems based upon it, she also has a renewed political vision – one based on the attempt to promote social justice. It is a vision which, like both Mouffe and Weeks, demands a form of commonality, solidarity, or sense of participating in the same society and yet which also celebrates heterogeneity and recognises specificity. As Chantal Mouffe argues, 'the question at stake is how to make our belonging to different communities of values, language and culture compatible with our common belonging to a political community whose rules we have to accept.'[22] Mouffe echoes the call of both Weeks and Young when she says that 'what we need is to envisage a form of commonality that respects diversity and makes room for different forms of individuality.'[23] If such a respect is absent, there is a danger that communities become divisive.

The creation of a radical pluralism will involve embracing solidarity and difference, a shift away from the concern with equality and sameness towards justice and difference. We can accept that cohesive communities are impossible ideals, abandon hope of perfect consensus and accept that dissent is inevitable, and yet also demand a grammar of conduct – a minimum shared sense of belonging as a basis for political co-existence.

Whilst many postmodern perspectives claim with increasing monotony to celebrate difference and diversity, the theorists here emphasise that actually to realise the 'possibility of political togetherness in difference',[24] we must construct and maintain systems of political inclusion and representation. To do so we need to recognise and analyse existing systems of oppression and injustice, and to create political structures which will begin to ameliorate their operation. In order to embark upon this route, we need a clearly formed and articulated set of values, ethical standpoints and evaluative criteria. As Young reveals, postmodernism has provided us with a basis for critiquing the logic of identity which denies or represses difference, resulting in hierarchical dichotomy. But if we are to argue for a system which allows for the clearer articulation of difference, in plural rather than dual form, we must do so from the basis of a theory of social justice.

Yet postmodernism frequently makes it more difficult to discuss questions of justice at all. As Jane Flax has noted: 'it is not clear that postmodernism has or could offer (a) positive vision(s) of justice.'[25] It offers little guide to the problems of how to resolve conflict among competing voices; how to effect a transition from the present in which many voices cannot speak, or are necessarily excluded, to a more polyvocal one; how to compensate for the political consequences of an unequal distribution and control of resources. The effect of the postmodern critique of universalism has all too often been to render any application of the concept of social justice problematic, leading to a political paralysis. This takes us into an impasse – and to increasing discontent. In the face of such immobility, theorists are beginning to resurrect the mobilising power of arguments about justice, to build a bridge between the supposed universalities of modernism and the fragmented particularities left behind by postmodernism.[26] 'Anything goes' is up for contestation; if not all manifestations of otherness are to be celebrated and fostered, principled positions are in need of political articulation and ethical justification.

It is both unnecessary and dangerous to assume that the

existence and practice of justice require a transcendental
grounding. We can accept the weak form of postmodernism and still maintain a legitimate concern with justice.
There is no absolute duality between grounding justice in
objective truth claims and giving up on it altogether.

David Harvey, by way of elaboration of this point,
reflects upon the current lack of political response to
exploitation. The face that 'raw class politics of an
exploitative sort' are all too often overlooked is in no small
part a product of the shift from universalism to
particularism. The very idea of a working class politics is
on the defensive, 'if not downright discredited in certain
"radical" circles,'[27] which focus on the fragmentation of
'progressive politics' around special issues and new social
movements. Once again we find the claim that: 'The effect
of the postmodern critique of universalism has been to
render any application of the concept of social justice
problematic.'[28]

It is often assumed that we have a simple dualistic
choice: to argue for a particular definition of social justice
through an invocation of higher order criteria which are
themselves in need of justification – and so embark upon a
metaphysical spiral in search of an absolute; or,
alternatively, to accept that social justice has no meaning
outside of discourse, that it means whatever individuals or
groups at some particular moment find it 'pragmatically,
instrumentally, emotionally, politically or ideologically
useful to mean.'[29] Harvey's implied argument here is that
whilst there are serious and important reasons for
recognising difference and refusing to apply principles
universally, the resultant 'infinite heterogeneity and
open-endedness about what justice might mean' leaves us
at best with a void, at worst with a very ugly state of affairs.

It is a wariness towards such false polarities which is at
the root of Harvey's worries about an appeal to
'unassimilated otherness' and the celebration of all
difference. For this invokes a form of relativism which is of
the 'anything goes' variety. In its place Harvey would have
us adopt a situatedness which internalises otherness, a
subjectivity which is constructed through its relations to

others. This relativism, Harvey argues, can be grounded in relations of social power. Similarly, Donna Haraway has argued that it is not difference that matters, but significant difference; and Deborah Rhode has stated that: 'Our focus needs to shift from difference to disadvantage and to the social conditions that perpetuate it.'[30] This is a situated or standpoint perspective; one which seeks to reveal the power relations within all discourses about justice. Harvey is therefore endorsing Nancy Hartsock's standpoint perspective, which she claims to be an alternative to 'the dead-end oppositions set up by post-modernism's rejection of the Enlightenment.'

This leaves Harvey endorsing the need for some form of (unspecified) epistemology which recognises some form of (unspecified) universals.[31] For if we are to reclaim the terrain of justice for progressive political purposes, we will need an epistemology that can distinguish between significant and insignificant differences or otherness, and can do so through an understanding of the social construction of situatedness. This argument is also to be found clearly articulated in the writing of an increasing number of theorists. For instance, Seyla Benhabib has also argued that the legacies of modernity require not wholesale dismantling but reconstruction and that 'a post-Enlightenment defence of universalism, without metaphysical props and historical conceits, is still viable.'[32] In other words, one can reject the metaphysical illusions of the Enlightenment whilst retaining a commitment to the universalist traditions of practical politics. Thus, echoing Hirst's assertion that there is no necessary absolute disjuncture between universalism and relativism, we could argue that such a universalism could be contextually sensitive and interactive. It is this assertion which distinguishes a reassertion of value from the restatement of personal preferences.

This move requires that the validity of truth claims is seen in terms of a discourse theory of justification, and a recognition that we are embodied and embedded selves whose identity is constructed narratively. Thus, whilst we may give up all use of foundational, essentialist, teleological and transcendental concepts, we will still need a notion of the self. And this theory of the self should not, as much postmodern feminist theory has argued, be one which insists on the self as simply a 'position in language' (Derrida) or an effect of discourse (Foucault). The self is not simply fictive, it is social, differentiated, embodied and historical.[33]

If we adopt this weak form of postmodernism, we can argue without contradiction for social justice, democratic pluralism and radical humanism. Hence Soper can call for a qualified defence of humanism; Young can argue that the primary aim of theorising is to promote social justice which involves 'guaranteeing individual civil and political rights, and guaranteeing that the basic needs of individual will be met so that they can freely pursue their own goals ...'.[34] And Weeks can call for a radical humanism, justified not through the metaphysical but through argument and debate.[35]

The postmodern engagements in, and preference for, fragmentation and differentiation have a quite serious, even normative, purpose: they serve to disrupt and erode the power of normalising discourses, they clear the space for the more disorderly and particular discourses of difference. But if these discourses of difference are to be articulated within a framework of justice, we must acknowledge that a postmodern politics must be concerned with concrete structures of power and normative expressions of value.

Judith Squires

Notes

[1] Seyla Benhabib, *Situating the Self*, Cambridge 1992, p 15.
[2] David Harvey in this collection p 114.
[3] Jane Flax in Gisela Bock and Susan James (eds), *Beyond Equality and Difference*, Routledge, London 1993, p 199.
[4] Kate Soper, this collection p 28.
[5] Jane Flax *Psychoanalysis, Feminism and Postmodernism in the Contemporary West*, University of California Press, Berkeley 1990, pp 32-34.
[6] Christopher Norris, this collection, p 186.
[7] For discussion of this point see Doreen Massey, 'A place called home?' in 'The Question of Home' *New Formations* issue no. 17 Summer 1992,

p 8. In this piece Massey notes that for all the talk of globalisation, flux and flow that characterises postmodern discourses, most of us still find ourselves waiting at a bus-stop for a bus that never comes. In other words the experiences meant to be characteristic of postmodernity are specific to a few.

[8] Stuart Hall, 'Minimal Selves', in *Identity*, ICA Documents no 6.

[9] For the distinction between strong and weak postmodernism see Seyla Benhabib *op cit*, pp 213-225. For discussion of 'soft sceptical' postmodernism see Nicholas Rengger 'No Time Like the Present? Postmodernism and Political Theory' in *Political Studies*, vol xl, no 3, September 1992, pp 561-570.

[10] Seyla Benhabib *op cit.*, p 224.

[11] Gayatri Spivak, 'An Interview', in *Radical Philosophy* Spring 1990, p 32.

[12] Kate Soper, this collection p 18.

[13] Spivak *op cit*, p 32.

[14] For a response to Baudrillard see Christopher Norris *Uncritical Theory*, Lawrence and Wishart, London 1992. Harvey's discussion is in this collection, p 85–94.

[15] Steven Connor, this collection, p 34.

[16] Chantel Mouffe, this collection, p 79.

[17] Jeffrey Weeks, this collection, p 195.

[18] *Ibid*, p 192.

[19] *Ibid*, p 198.

[20] Iris Marion Young this collection, p 127.

[21] *Ibid*, p 135.

[22] Chantal Mouffe, p 80.

[23] *Ibid*, p 81.

[24] Mouffe, p 81; Weeks, p 203; Young, p 135.

[25] Jane Flax in Bock and James (eds), Routledge, London 1993, p 198.

[26] Harvey, this collection, p 102.

[27] *Ibid*, p 93–4.

[28] *Ibid*, p 95.

[29] *Ibid*, p 96.

[30] Deborah Rhode, in Bock and James (eds), p 158.

[31] Harvey, this collection, p 112.

[32] Seyla Benhabib, *op cit*, p 5.

[33] See Benhabib, *op cit*, p 3; see also Flax (1992), Rosi Braidotti, *Patterns of Dissonance*, Polity, Cambridge 1991.

[34] Young, this collection, p 136.

[35] Weeks, this collection, p 195.

Beyond Relativism and Objectivism

Postmodernism, Subjectivity and the Question of Value

KATE SOPER

Of late, there has been a certain amount of discussion within circles influenced by, and sympathetic to, postmodernist critical approaches as to how far these can consistently defer engagement with traditional criteria of truth and value. It has been suggested that the eclecticism and relativist logic of postmodernism is inherently self-stultifying, or at any rate incompatible with the defence of these modes of cognition as offering some form of political and cultural enlightenment. They hence deliver their advocates into a condition of theoretical paralysis, in which they can neither argue for the 'truth' or knowledge status of the forms of argument through which they have exposed the mistakes and self-delusions of foundationalist metaphysics, nor lay claim to any emancipatory values in liberating a left politics from the disquieting assimilations of identity concealed within its collectivist and humanist 'grand narrative'.

This 'impasse', it should be said, does not necessarily afflict deconstructive strategies in themselves (except in the sense that it can always be asked of their practitioners what motivates them if not an impulse to get us to think aright about texts, or at any rate to perceive what the text itself is blind to). For to pursue the path of Derridean *différance* is strictly speaking to preempt the appeal to the 'identities' whose alleged occlusion by orthodox liberal or socialist discourse has been invoked in justification of the Anglo-American use of deconstructive methods.[1] Thus it might be argued that Derridean theory, in openly acknowledging its self-subverting quality (that it can rely only on what it theorises as non-reliable), is neither self-subverting nor non-self-subverting – though I think it must also be the condition of so arguing that it can lend itself neither to this politics, nor to that, neither to value commitments nor to their disowning.

Some of my argument in what follows does bear on the general question of the acceptability of the Derridean position/non-position though, insofar as it does, I present this precisely as a question of 'which way to jump'; in other words, I present it as a problem of the incommensurability of certain thought 'paradigms' and not as a problem of the internal consistency of either. But what I shall be mainly addressing here are certain issues concerning value and subjectivity which arise in virtue of the attempt to jump both ways, to have, as it were, a foot both in and out of deconstruction. They are issues which present themselves, and have recently become a focus of postmodernist self-criticism, as a result of the various ways in which post-modernist ideas have been yoked into the service of a leftwing politics or have been defended as emancipatory insights. (And these ideas, I should add, are by no means of exclusively Derridean origin, but often in fact owe more to theorists of whom Derrida has been critical, such as Foucault, or to the progress sceptical and ironic self-positionings recommended by thinkers like Lyotard and Rorty).[2]

One, rather shorthand, way of talking about these issues has been in terms of a postmodernist 'suppression' of values, and its refusal to employ an associated vocabulary (in aesthetics of 'judgement', 'artistic worth', 'intrinsic merit', etc; in ethics of 'rights', 'freedom', 'duty', etc; and in epistemology of 'truth', 'verification', 'objectivity', etc). But in fact this is a somewhat misleading shorthand, since postmodernist argument has invited us not so much to suppress this vocabulary but to construe it as directing us to nothing beyond or outside its own discourse. There are, according to this position, no transcendent, extra-discursive qualities or experiences to which we can appeal as the grounds for the talk of values and the discriminations it offers, since these refer us only to what discourse itself constructs. The dispute, in short, has to do with how far we retain or sever a discursive – non-discursive dialectic; with how far the 'text' or 'discourse' of values is what it is in virtue of how the 'world' is, how far we read the world to be as it is only in virtue of the discourse or text. This means that if the symptoms of a return of the 'repressed' of value are now disturbing the psychic composure of certain postmodernist modes of reflection, then this is not to do with the repression of a vocabulary but to do with the repression or evasion of the realist commitments which may be essential to sustaining any consistent argument about values.

If this, then, is the controversy or point of tension, at issue, it seems appropriate that I should begin by saying something about where I stand in regard to it, and I shall do this – for strategic purposes which should become clearer as I proceed – by invoking a caricature of the dispute. The caricature presents us on the one side with the dogged metaphysicians, a fierce and burly crew, stalwartly defending various bedrocks and foundations by means of an assortment of trusty but clankingly mechanical concepts such as 'class', 'materialism', 'human-ism', 'literary merit', 'transcendence' and so forth. Obsolete as these weapons are, they have the one distinct advantage that in all the dust thrown up by the flailing around with them, their wielders do not realise how seldom they connect with the opposition. On the other side stands the opposition, the feline ironists and revellers in relativism, dancing lightheartedly upon the waters of *différance*, deflecting all foundationalist blows with an adroitly directed ludic laser beam. Masters of situationist strategy, they side-step the heavy military engagement by refusing to do anything but play.

Now, if I were allowed only the mirror of this caricature in which to find a reflection of my own position, I would be feeling pretty schizoid, but I guess in the end I would have to recognise something minimally less distorting of my own features in the grotesque metaphysical Cerberus than in the ironical Cheshire grin. In other words, if forced to align myself in terms of this caricature, I am ready to do so, provided that in exchange everything further I have to say be received as typical of the growlings of the monstrous metaphysicians.

First, then, a few growlings about the equivocal feelings which our postmodern times can induce – an equivocation which at its most extreme could be compared to that of the third century Chinese poet, Chuang Chou, who tells us that one night he dreamt he was a butterfly, but on awakening did not know whether he had dreamt he was a butterfly or whether he was not now a butterfly dreaming he was Chuang Chou. For at times it can seem as if we stand at the interface of two incommensurable modes of thinking, each of which, we know, should we yield to it, has the capacity to constitute itself as reality and the other as its dream or myth. Each, in other words, seems possessed of such a drug-like power to re-orchestrate our mental outlook that we hesitate to lend ourselves as guinea pigs to either of its thought experiments.

At one level – that at which we are called upon to decide our general affective response to the 'postmodern' condition – we can think of this equivocation in terms of the emotional tug between two contrary invitations. One asks us to keep a grip on the horror and ugliness of our world, never to forget the extent to which it is beset by war, famine, torture, loss of nature, grotesque inequalities and intolerable oppressions, and which therefore calls upon us to analyse all practice and historical process in terms of the degree to which it promotes or detracts from the realisation of greater peace, equality, democracy, ecologi-cal well-being and the future flourishing of our species and its planet. The other is the invitation to view history as littered with the victims of such well intentioned visions and utopian projects, and in the light of that to give ourselves over to a pragmatic acceptance of the loss of values – an acceptance, moreover, which we might as well feel as cheerful about as we can. For if utopias are never to be realised, is there any more harm to be done in accepting their loss than in lamenting it? This, then, is the invitation to respond to dystopia by a consciously decadent pleasuring in its awfulness. It is – as Elizabeth Wilson has suggested – to convert 'leftwing' anxiety into a solution: to live in a film noir world.[3]

Now it is debatable how far the flight into cinema and the film noir option has exerted any very real attraction even among the more committed adherents of postmodernist anti-progressivism. But if there are some who have sensed the temptation of decadence, but yet hesitated to succumb to it, they will be aware, I think, that any hesitations in this area are such as to draw them back into the camp of the metaphysicians. If they hesitate, I suggest, it is because they know that the allure of a pragmatic dystopianism is a fantasy in which it is much easier to cocoon oneself if one is already enjoying comforts which figure only in the utopian dreams of the African peasant, street child in Rio di Janiero or Iraqi political prisoner. They know, in other words, that revelling in the loss of progress is a Western metropolitan privilege which depends on living in a certain state of grace, a condition where no one is starving you, no one torturing you, no one even denying you the price of a cinema ticket or tube fare to the conference on postmodernism.

My first point, then, is this. We should accept the implication of any equivocation that is felt about yielding to postmodernist cynicism, namely, that it speaks to a certain sensitivity about the self-indulgent quality of that reaction – to an awareness of how parochial it really is to present the loss of hope or progress as if it were a universally available mode of adjustment to the ugliness of our times. But to recognise this, is in effect to be forced out of equivocation back into open commitment to certain political principles and values. It is to recognise certain objective structures of oppression by reference to which we discriminate between practices, dispute the wisdom of various emancipatory strategies, and, indeed, engage in more than theory.

But, to come back now to the theoretical opposition

whose caricature I sketched in my opening remarks, where a similar point holds: on the one hand, we have grounded theory, a cognitive position which remains committed to truth and objectivity as the condition of making sense of value preference; on the other hand, we have deconstruction and difference theory, a perspective from which all appeals to intrinsic quality as the ground of aesthetic and cultural judgement, or to objectively verifiable needs and sufferings as the justification of political and ethical commitments, must be rejected as so many forms of logocentrism, as resting their claims on appeals to concepts of truth and value which are radically indecidable, unstable metaphors always intruding between the presence or state of affairs they supposedly grasp. Here too there is extensive equivocation, and precisely because one can appreciate the measure of virtue in both approaches. But again, I would want to argue that the very reasoning which allows us to appreciate the attractions and importance of discourse theory and deconstruction is such as to commit the reasoner to defending certain values.

Why, for example, lend ourselves to the politics of 'difference' if it is not in virtue of its enlightenment? – what it permits in the way of releasing subjects from the conflations of imperialising discourse and the constructed identities of binary oppositions? Why lend ourselves to the deconstruction of the liberal humanist rhetoric, if not to expose the class or racial or gender identities it occluded? Why challenge truth if not in the interests of revealing the potentially manipulative powers of the discourses which have attained to the status of knowledge? Why call science in question if not, in part, because of the military and ecological catastrophes to which the blind pursuit of its instrumental rationality has delivered us? Why problematise the artistic canon and its modes of aesthetic discrimination, if not because we wish to draw attention to the ways in which art can collude with the values of the establishment and serve to reinforce its power elites? In other words, insofar as we want to cling to some of the insights of poststructuralist theory, we seem caught up in ways of explaining and justifying this inclination in terms which, strictly speaking, only make sense if we are prepared to defend certain forms of truth, ethical value and political principle.

All this could be rephrased in the form of a critique of the inconsistency of postmodernist critique: an inconsistency which, if brought to the surface, would seem to blur any clear-cut demarcation between the relativists and realists, ironists and metaphysicians. One, moreover, could illustrate this inconsistency as it surfaces in respect of a number of differing concerns or domains of theoretical engagement. I shall here explore the idea a little further with reference to cultural value and the position of the subject.

We know, I think, how important deconstructive approaches in cultural criticism have been in illuminating the ways in which appeal to the 'freedom' and transcendent values of the artistic work can screen out consideration of its ideological function – preserve it from the scrutiny of the political values it may sustain, however unconsciously. An exclusive concern with the formal and aesthetic value of cultural production can in this sense legitimate various forms of reaction and elitism, and allow the critic to ward off all minority challenges to the canon by dismissing them as politically – therefore improperly – motivated. As Christopher Lasch has put it, 'the more intellectual purity identifies itself with "value-free" investigations, the more it empties of political content, the easier it is for public officials to tolerate it. This gains the co-operation of writers, teachers and artists not as paid propagandists or state-censored time servers, but as so-called "free" intellectuals capable of policing their own jurisdictions'.[4]

So far so good. But if we ask in whose interests we are deconstructing this notion of aesthetic value and cultural freedom, we shall almost certainly be referred by the critic to all those marginalised or minority identities (women, blacks, sexual and ethnic groupings, etc) who have been colonised or suppressed in the name of the purity of art. We may also be told that it is to allow popular tastes and interests to be released from the puritanism or condescension of the elitist value commitments. The problem, however, is that such justifications paradoxically invoke the cultural and judgemental freedom they deny. For unless we arbitarily call a halt to the logic of discourse theory, why should we not deny the freedom of these liberated 'identities', why not view them in turn as the unconscious agents of someone else's cultural policing, as themselves constructed subjects who are blind to the propagandist purposes they are serving in the discourse which claims their liberation?[5]

Furthermore, unless critics are prepared to engage in aesthetic discrimination concerning the intrinsic quality of cultural production, it is difficult to see why they are so keen to challenge the canonical status of certain works or to lay claim to the preserve of 'high' art. Unless we think there is something unique about art, that it has special powers to move and excite and illuminate, then why enter into any ideological contest over it? Why be any less happy to let its established practitioners be the guardians of its standards than we are, say, in the case of mathematics? The answer, surely, is that we *do* think art is distinctive in being reducible neither to a matter of formal skills and achievements, nor to a matter of ideology and cultural history. To put the point crudely, if we want to claim art for 'our' politics, it is in virtue of its possessing qualities and standards internal to itself and demanding a specific aesthetic appraisal. To go forward, then, from the insight shed by deconstructive strategies we need *both* to defend the political and ethical values underpinning these, *and* to relate these to value commitments of a more purely formal character. Because in the end, I think, what we are about here is wanting more people to have access to the liberation and particular pleasures of high quality cultural production. We are talking about cultural strategies which implicitly aim at the development of a more acute and educated aesthetic sensibility within a political programme where this is conceived as an integral component of self-realisation and cultural emancipation.

Clearly all these considerations bear very directly on the question of the subject, a site where all the lurking inconsistencies of the post-structuralist approach tend to converge; and a site, in a sense, where we feel this most intensely because it is reflected very directly in our own psychical experience. What I mean by this is that, even as we acknowledge ourselves to be de-centred and fragmented subjectivities, the gendered constructs of patriarchy and mouthpieces of a discursive ventriloquism, we also seem to rediscover a centre, the existential, angst-ridden self who must also make sense of it, and seek to reorganise desire, re-read the world, adjust behaviour, and so on, in the light of that awareness. As anti-humanist approaches present us as splintered, we feel a very humanist splintering between the self who acknowledges the Freudian or feminist challenge to autonomy, and the self who feels called upon to act as a morally responsible agent of self-change.

It may be objected that I am speaking here only to the experience of a handful of academics and left-wing intellectuals, and that this provides no basis for any more general claims about contemporary forms of self-appraisal. This is true in the sense that only they are likely to acknowledge and articulate the theoretical sources of any change in perspective. But I think it would be mistaken all the same to underestimate the extent of the influence of psychoanalysis and feminism in bringing about a broader shift of approach to questions of self-knowledge, and indeed in generating what we may regard as a fairly universal but specifically modern reflexivity in attitudes to self-hood. Thus it would seem difficult to account for the depth and scope of the revolution in thinking occasioned by feminism without assuming a fairly extensive 'anti-humanist' conception of the self as the involuntary construct of gender conventions to which one had previously been relatively blind, and indeed had not experienced as conventions at all, but rather as some natural dimension of personality. Psychoanalysis, for its part, can be said to have influenced an appraisal of one's adult life in the light of childhood formation which is by no means confined to those familiar with Freud's writings. Insofar, moreover, as feminism has

itself employed psychoanlytic insights in directing attention to the effect of 'mother-dominated' nurturing,
oedipal responses and the symbolic order of patriarchy on
gender formation, it has tended to complement the
Freudian retrospection on the role of infantile experience
in determining adult responses.

This is not to suggest that pre-Freudian culture did not
engage in quite considered reflections of this kind (one has
only to recall Wordsworth's 'Immortality' ode or Mill's
Autobiography to acknowledge this); nor is it to suggest that
there is not a certain pre- and post-Freudian continuity in
their quality. But there is a break, too, (marked perhaps
most notably by a loss of the sense of childhood as 'lost
innocence'); certainly, I think, we have seen the emergence
of a specifically modern scepticism or diffidence about the
extent to which the individual can invoke his or her
conscious experience as if it were the whole of what could
be known about the self – as if this form of self-knowledge
were exhaustive of everything that could feasibly enter
into an expression of individuality.

If this is the case, then I think it can also be argued that
it introduces a rather particular form of ethical
self-awareness, and that this paradoxically invites a more
'humanist' understanding of agency and self-change, even
as it derives its quality from the 'anti-humanist'
perspectives we bring to bear on ourselves. The particular
tension here has to do with the fact that if we recognise
ourselves to be the 'constructs' of *social* forces, we can no
longer so readily appeal to *nature* (that is, to our
personality or to how we just 'happen' to be ...) as the
obstacle to self-change. We have become, one might say,
more alert to the fact that the appeal to the 'naturality' of
the emotions lodged in our breast is not only no 'excuse'
for them, but itself quite possibly to be viewed as a
manifestation of our resistance to altering them. In this
sense, we may feel an existentialist responsibility to
changing the social forces through which we acknowledge
ourselves to have been 'constructed'; but at the same time –
and here is the rub – in recognising the extent to which we
are 'constructed' selves, we also recognise and pay due

heed to all those reasons why we are so resistant to altering our ways and may indeed not manage to achieve it however hard we try. In other words, we frequently confront situations where an acute sense of responsibility for self-change goes together with a no less acute understanding of why this cannot be viewed simply in terms of an existential project, and why it would be too purely voluntaristic to suppose that it could. Anyone, for example (in other words almost all of us to some degree or other), who has been caught up in the transformation of attitudes to gender and sexuality which has been the consequence of feminism, will know that what makes the adjustment of behaviour peculiarly fraught in this area is not so much any overt ideological resistance to feminist demands, but relates rather to a tension between these 'autonomous' and 'non-autonomous' moments of self-hood. The 'identities' we seek to change (and which in changing we know ourselves to be contributing to changes in the conventions through which identity is constructed) are also those we cannot entirely over-ride, and whose desires it would be quite pointless to attempt to ignore.

These tensions, moreover, have their particular effects not only in respect of the ethics of self-change, but also on the considerations we bring to bear in determining what is moral in our responses to the behaviour of others. In other words, they present us with dilemmas which are indisputably ethical in character, but also very much the product of current discourse and understanding, and therefore to be viewed as historically relative – as, for example, when we are placed in situations which invite quite different behavioural responses depending whether we view them in the light of feminist or psychoanalytic perspectives or approach them more conventionally, as situations involving free agents whose conscious expressions of feeling demand our sympathy, and come with certain entitlements to respect. How far should we be prepared to cause offence or pain to others (especially where our relations with them are particularly sensitive, as with parents or friends) by exposing, say, their unconscious sexism? When a father asserts his parental authority in disciplining his children, is he bringing them up well or reaffirming patriarchal power? How far should we view our adult affections as the freely bestowed gifts of one autonomous subject upon another, how far as the legacy of infantile needs, dependencies and aggressions?

Such questions are complex, posed quite possibly in terms which many would want to contest, and I can do no more than gesture at them here. But a summary way of stating them might be to say that anti-humanist challenges to the sovereign subject have permitted forms of self-scrutiny and awareness which seem both liberating and essential to the establishment of better human relations; but these are also unsettling, precisely because of their de-sanctifying effect on former conceptions of love and sexuality, because they seem an obstacle to a more unthinking and spontaneous affective and erotic response, and because of the particular nature of the ethical demands with which they confront us. Of course, I recognise that this summary statement is saturated with humanistic value assumptions. But how else can I state it? How else can a metaphysician like myself give voice to her equivocations?

But finally, let me shift from talking about equivocations and inconsistencies to talking about what these may imply by way of a need for a post-post-structuralist programme in which we acknowledge more openly the latent metaphysical dependencies of the critical attempt to suppress value, without giving up on the gains which that critical move has brought us. What is at issue here is the possibility of a more synthetic approach which combines alertness to the deficiencies and crudeness of much traditional value discourse with alertness to the self-defeating quality of the attempt to avoid all principled positions in theory. This would be a kind of Kantian programme in the sense that it would involve a critique of pure value: it would submit the 'transcendental signifiers' to the scrutiny of sceptical and relativist appraisals in order to acquire a better sense of the minimal value commitments essential to sustain the critical power of social and cultural theory. It would involve giving up on the grand narrative idea of a single truth, without giving up on the idea of truth as a regulative ideal, something we should be working to attain to in all our behaviours and critical responses. It would insist on bringing judgements of quality to cultural production without allowing that the traditional formal values of 'high' art provide their only criteria. It would acknowledge the constructed nature of subjectivity without supposing that this makes all humanist questions of ethics and agency redundant. I believe it is only an approach of this kind that will prevent a roll-back reaction. In other words, I think it is only by means of a re-engagement with values, which is informed and tempered by the rationalities which tended to their suppression, that a healthy postmodernist self-criticism does not revert to an unhealthy legitimation of the unreconstructed modes of thinking that were the just target of initial attack.

Of course, I recognise that there is a riposte to all this which is a kind of last laugh at the very idea that inconsistency or self-subversion could worry a mode of reflection which had cut loose from the logic of logocentrism. Only an old fashioned metaphysician who had failed to undersand the full disruption to the values of consistency which had been wrought by the critique of presence, could think that she could trouble a difference theory perspective or reclaim it for value by pointing to its self-subverting quality.

This, certainly, is the real impasse, the interface where the flip over from dream to reality occurs – where one mentality stands poised to swallow the other. But it is also the point where I shall emit a last growl to the effect that there is then no point in communing any further.

Notes

[1] Though opinions differ as to how far Derrida himself escapes a 'philosophy of origins' or the prejudices of 'identity-thinking'. Thus Peter Dews has argued (*Logics of Disintegration*, Verso, London, 1987, Chap. 1) that Derrida is returned to this perspective in making *différance* the generative ground of identity; and that in making 'the fatal slide towards an account of difference as logically prior to and

constitutive of identity' he 'generates insoluble problems for his philosophy' (p 42).

[2] Full bibliographies of these thinkers are readily available and would seem inappropriate in the context of a brief appraisal of this kind. I refer here particularly to the argument of Lyotard's *The Postmodern Condition*, Manchester 1986 and Rorty's *Contingency, Irony and Solidarity*, Cambridge 1989. Derrida criticizes Foucault in 'Cogito and the History of Madness' (*Writing and Difference*, London 1978); for a recent discussion of their respective positions (which argues, however, that they tend to agreement on questions of power and ethics), see R. Boyne, *Foucault and Derrida: the Other Side of Reason*, London 1990.

[3] In a talk given to a conference at Kent University on 'Feminism and Postmodernism'.

[4] Christopher Lasch, *The Agony of the American Left*, London 1970, pp 94-5. See Alan Sinfield's discussion, *Literature, Politics and Culture in Postwar Britain*, Oxford 1989, pp 102-5. I would like to acknowledge a debt in my thinking on these issues to Michèle Barratt's discussion of aesthetic value in *Women's Oppression Today*, Verso, London 1980, and to Terry Eagleton's *The Function of Criticism*, Verso, London 1984 and his chapter on 'Marxism and Aesthetic Value' in *Criticism and Ideology*, Verso, London 1976.

[5] This is not in any sense to imply that challenges to the canon should not be made, nor that those who make them do so on what they explicitly recognise to be non-aesthetic grounds – on the grounds, for example, that works should be studied because they represent minority interests. My point, rather, is that the justifications for such non-aesthetic criteria may ultimately rely, at a more implicit level, on arguments which tend to undermine those invoked by critics like Lasch when they query art's claims to autonomy.

The Necessity of Value

STEVEN CONNOR

Value is inescapable. This is not to be taken as a claim for
the objective existence or categorical force of any values or
imperatives in particular; but rather as a claim that the
processes of estimating, ascribing, modifying, affirming
and even denying value, in short, the processes of
evaluation, can never be avoided. We are claimed always
and everywhere, by the necessity of value in this active,
transactional sense. Seen in this way, the play of value is
bound up intimately with motivation and purpose of every
kind. No one has put this point more emphatically in
recent years than John Fekete, so I may gratefully borrow
his words:

> Not to put too fine a point on it, we live, breathe, and
> excrete values. No aspect of human life is unrelated to
> values, valuations and validations. Value orientations and
> value relations saturate our experiences and life practices
> from the smallest established microstructures of feeling,
> thought and behaviour to the largest established macro-
> structures of organizations and institutions. The history of
> cultures and social formations is unintelligible except in
> relation to a history of value orientations, value ideals,
> goods values, value responses, and value judgements, and
> their objectivisations, interplay, and transformations.[1]

And yet, the most striking thing about the critical and
interpretative theory which has flourished in the
humanities and social sciences over the last decade or so

31

has been the decisive swing away from a concern with judgement and value and towards a concern with meaning and interpretation. It is this concern that holds together and provides an institutional identity for the otherwise striking diversity of the forms of contemporary literary theory, for instance. What hermeneutics, reader-centred criticism, semiotic analysis, discourse-theory, psychoanalytic theory, new historicism, deconstruction and all the varieties of politically-accented criticism which draw on the former perspectives, Marxism, feminism, gay and ethnic critical discourse have in common, is their focus on the activities of knowing, understanding, decoding and interpreting. Even forms of criticism which might be expected to ask other kinds of question instead of, or alongside, the questions 'what does it mean?' or 'how do we know what it means?', and indeed proclaim their independence from such questions, are drawn in by the force of the interpretative paradigm.

Barbara Herrnstein Smith ascribes this 'exile of evaluation' within the literary academy especially to the predominance of linguistic models, and a lack of familiarity with disciplines such as sociology and economics in which questions of value have a central place.[2] But, quite apart from the dubious accuracy of this assessment (the association between literature and sociology has been strong, if intermittent, over the last few decades), this does not adequately account for the exile of evaluation in the disciplines of the humanities, since it does not really explain why linguistic models and theories have come to exercise this dominance. The reason for this lies, I believe, in the increasing professionalisation and institutionalisation of the disciplines of the humanities and, more generally, the multiplication of the forms in which culture is socially managed and mediated. In the universities and institutions of learning, this professionalisation was first encouraged by the expansion of higher education in the societies of the developed West during the 1960s and subsequently reinforced and, surprisingly, even accelerated by the assaults on the humanities mounted by successive governments in Britain and the USA during the

1980s. For what these assaults amounted to was a rejection of the concept of an evaluative discipline in favour of a positivist and instrumentalist model of education as training, a model which was itself derived from a narrowly idealised version of scientific and technical education, in which facts, knowledge and interpretation have an ascendancy over values and the processes of value-judgement. Seen in this way, the retreat from evaluation in the disciplines of the humanities is a kind of protective colouring, an attempt to conform to a newly dominant paradigm of research and education. (Not, of course, that this apparent retreat from evaluation is itself anything other than a powerful transvaluation of cultural value.)

But this is far from being the most striking paradox about this situation. For if the dominance of interpretative critical theory during the last two decades has been achieved at the cost of exiling evaluation, then it is also conspicuously the case that this has been a period in which the force of value in the humanities has been felt unmissably and ubiquitously, a period in which Fredric Jameson can declare with justice that the prevailing mode of criticism is in fact the ethical.[3] Indeed, when one considers the kinds of question which have driven critical theory and practice through the 1970s and the decade that has followed Jameson's judgement – the politics of interpretation and representation, the prejudiced representation of minority groups in literature and art, the violent effects of discourse, and the question of the social effects and functions of cultural practices of all kinds – one does seem forced to acknowledge that there seems to have been an intensification rather than a waning of ethical and evaluative concerns.

How, then, are we to reconcile this with Barbara Herrnstein Smith's uncompromising judgement that 'the entire problematic of value and evaluation has been evaded and explicitly exiled' in contemporary theory (*Contingencies of Value*, p 17)? One explanation of what is happening in literary and cultural disciplines might be that critical theory, especially in its adversary forms such as feminism, Marxism or the varieties of politically-accented deconstruction, has turned away from what are newly experienced as unacceptably narrow and implausible views of the value of literary and cultural works, and especially that view associated with artistic modernism which suggests that the only true value of art is a value intrinsic to itself. On this view, critical theory would have rejected, not the idea of value as such, but the notion of aesthetic value as autotelic and self-determining. The most sophisticated and convincing political objections to this notion of aesthetic value argue not so much that this notion is inaccurate as that it masks and perpetuates certain very definite relations of power, such that the notion of pure and non-negotiable aesthetic value always has a nonaesthetic exchange-value in political and economic terms. The resulting critique of aesthetic ideology is therefore, strictly speaking, not a critique of the notion of value, or a denial of the possibility of evaluation in general, but a rejection of the unjustly limiting forms which aesthetic evaluation has taken.[4] Such critics are restoring the authority of the question 'what is this text/artefact/practice good *for?*', against the modernist question 'what is it good *as?*'; they are asking 'what good is it?' as well as 'how good is it?'.

But, if we accept that the rise of postmodern theory involves such a shift from a restricted to an expanded economy of value, we have still to account for a reluctance on the part of much theory to speak of, or theorise the question of value itself. There is no shortage of evaluations and evaluative positions and commitments (probably there never is), but there continues to be a failure to open out the question of value to theory on its own terms, or to talk about the question of value other than sceptically, embarrassedly or partially. Given the everywhere-detectible force of ethical and evaluative motivations in contemporary cultural theory, the frailty of attempts to subject this force to enquiry is truly striking. In the light of this, we might offer a refinement of Barbara Herrnstein Smith's judgement and suggest that value and evaluation have not so much been exiled, as driven into the critical unconscious, where they continue to exercise force but without being available for analytic scrutiny.

The evidence of this is to be found in the shape and form of many of the recurrent debates within feminism, Marxism and cultural studies. For feminism, the most complex and recurrent problem in recent years has surely been how to reconcile an oppositional politics grounded in the idea of a distinctive and victimised female identity with a politics that criticises the fetishistic and oppressive notion of identity as traditionally constituted. A similar problem recurs in contemporary Marxist debates, in which the critique of false totalisations and absolutisms must find a way to stop short of dissolving its own claims to provide a total or encompassing grand narrative of oppression and emancipation. The various forms of cultural study, especially ethnic and post-colonial critical theory, which draw on Foucault's critique of universalist notions of the human, must similarly find a way of balancing a liberal and progressive antihumanism against the regressive forms of antihumanism so rife in the world today. All of these problems involve an interesting unwillingness or failure to engage theoretically with the problem of value, and this may be said partly to account for their recalcitrance. In each of these areas, the ethical-evaluative impulse is to be found in a practice of *negative interpretation*, in the impulse to liquefy certain violent or oppressive coagulations of value (the mistaking of white, or male culture for culture in general, the priority of élite culture over popular culture, the centring of history around narrowly reductive categories and subjects, and so on), which leads to a suspicion of value and evaluation in general, as though the operations associated with the transaction of value were always destined to lead to (unjust) hierarchy and (violent) exclusion. The notion of value in this situation can become the object of a superstitious dread and induce a state of neurotic dependency, in which the feared or despised object (the notion of fixed meaning, or unified identity, metaphysics, the grand narrative) is repeatedly and obsessively invoked in order to be revoked.

The problem is, then, that for a theory that depends upon negative interpretation, on an essentially hygienic practice of extricating itself from error, delusion and ideology, the category of value along with the practices of evaluation may seem to be contaminated all the way through. But value, like the unconscious, tolerates no negativity, since every negative evaluation, even of the practice of evaluation itself, must always constitute a kind of evaluation on its own terms, even if it implies or states no positive alternative value. Theory of any kind, but perhaps especially a theory driven by an ethic of extrication and embodied in negative interpretation, is always steeped in value, and always asks the question of value in a particularly intense form. A period in which values are profoundly in question is always equally a period of energetic value-formation. But a situation in which the energy of ethical disidentification is unmatched by an attention to the nature of ethics and value themselves, in which it has become difficult to be explicit about the question of value, is a strange and dangerous one indeed.

One response to this might be that it is neither necessary nor desirable to be explicit about the question of value; that such explicitness belongs, not to the critic, but to the legislator. Indeed, the critique of rationality and all its associated psychopolitical apparatuses offered by contemporary theory might seem to compromise precisely the possibility of a rational grasping of the nature of value implied by the ideal of such explicitness. The various versions of such a critique need to be taken very seriously indeed, but it is precisely their force and seriousness, which is to say, the rational and ethical claims that they exercise, that reveals them to be value-claims in themselves, imperatives which loop back to the problem of the expression and constraining of value in contemporary critical discourse.

We have seen that the replacement of evaluation with interpretation is one way of enacting such a constraint. There are also two others, which, depressingly enough, seem to be characteristic of most of the attempts to return to the question in recent years. The first is the impulse to uphold, return to, or orientate oneself towards stable or

absolute forms of value. The second (and it may seem
surprising to characterise this as a constraint rather than
an expansion of the question of value) is the desire to
tolerate the maximum of competing values. Insofar as the
first attitude depends upon the idea of absolute values,
which lie above and beyond the play of transaction and
relativity, it may be said to favour values as objects over
evaluative processes, or, in terms of a distinction once
offered by John Dewey, to favour 'prizing' over
'appraising'.[5] Such a view will typically regard it as the
purpose of evaluation to escape from or get beyond
evaluative processes, in order to 'arrive' at evaluative
outcomes. The second, more pluralistic attitude will tend,
on the contrary, to favour the continuation or enabling of
evaluative processes, as against the attempt to preserve,
discover or derive particular values. This second attitude
may be embodied for example in Jean-François Lyotard's
notion that justice consists in 'the possibility of continuing
to play the game of the just', and is that which allows 'that
the question of the just and the unjust be, and remain,
raised'.[6] A familiar version of the opposition between the
two attitudes is the standoff between metaphysics versus
différance, as presented in this collection by Kate Soper: on
the one hand, there is 'a fierce and burly crew, stalwartly
defending various bedrocks and foundations by means of
an assortment of trusty but clankingly mechanical
concepts such as "class", "materialism", "humanism",
"literary merit", "transcendence" and so forth' and, on the
other, 'the feline ironists and revellers in relativism,
dancing lightheartedly upon the waters of *différance*,
deflecting all foundationalist blows with an adroitly
directed ludic laser beam'.[7] This is a self-confessed
caricature; but, as we will see later on, it is hard to
characterise the opposition between these two modes, the
absolutising and the relativising of value, in any way that
does not implicitly confirm one or other side of the issue,
one or other evaluation of the question of value itself.

A greater ethical curtailment than these two forms of
constraint in themselves is the limiting exclusiveness of the
binarism they form together, which makes it impossible to

imagine a theory of value which does not either propose some absolute closure or some absolute openness, monolithic fixation or slithering difference. But there is in fact no choice, or possibility of choice between these two alternatives, between the role of legislator and critic. No negative critique, even in the sveltest, most ironic form, is imaginable without investment in or assumption of alternative values; while, on the other hand, the assertion of absolute value always brings with it a vulnerability to critique in terms of the absolute value proposed. Scepticism about metanarratives is impossible except as instructed by the hypothesis of some juster, more inclusive metanarrative, measured against which the suspected metanarrative falls short; while, on the other side, the assertion of a metanarrative must always leave open, in the name of its very claim total inclusiveness, the possibility of its discrediting. The structure of value is therefore paradoxical, involving the simultaneous desire and necessity to affirm unconditional values and the desire and necessity of subjecting such values to continuous, corrosive scrutiny.

To date, discussions of value in critical theory have simplified this paradoxical structure into an *either/or: either* absolute value *or* relativism; *either* fixity *or* play. I want to look at one side of this antinomy, as it is presented in what might be called the 'radical-pragmatist' account of value of Barbara Herrnstein Smith, in order to show the interinvolvement of the two dimensions of value. Smith's powerful argument in *Contingencies of Value* is simply stated: everything participates in value, but nowhere in the world or out of it are there to be found any unfalsifiable use-values, transcendent aesthetic values, or ultimate moral goods. She cheerfully accepts the principle which has been so horrifying to many moral philosophers, that there are no statements of value, or evaluations, which are not statements of particular needs, desires or preferences, whether of individuals, or of groups. This means that it makes no sense to speak of the truth or not of moral or evaluative statements. *This is good* is always in fact a variant of the statement *I like this*, or *I value this*. All values are entirely contingent, always in the process of being transacted in the multiple, overlapping economies of needs, desires and wants which make up human life and history. Although there are certain limited forms of regularity in the patterns of social evaluation in particular cultural groups, Smith urges a view of the fundamental 'scrappiness' or heterogeneity of human needs, interests and goals, which can consequently never be concentrated or simplified into any single principle of value:

> There is ... no way for individual or collective choices, practices, activities, or acts, 'economic' or otherwise, to be ultimately summed-up, compared, and evaluated: neither by the single-parameter hedonic calculus of classic utilitarianism, nor by the most elaborate multiple-parameter formulas of contemporary mathematical economics, nor by any inversion and presumptive transcendence of either. There is no way to give a reckoning that is simultaneously total and final. There is no Judgement Day. There is no *bottom* bottom line anywhere, for anyone or for 'man'. (p 149)

One of the most striking manoeuvres employed by Smith is her assault on what she incisively calls the 'Egalitarian Fallacy', the belief that in a system in which no values can be shown to have final or absolute authority, in which no values can be shown to be finally true, rather than merely powerfully or widely believed, all values must therefore be equal. But to acknowledge 'that no value judgement can be more "valid" than another *in the sense of* an objectively truer statement of the objective value of an object', in no way disallows the possibility of making meaningful value-judgements. It is just that the value of these value-judgements 'must be understood, evaluated, and compared *otherwise*, that is, as something other than "truth value" or "validity" in the objectivist, essentialist sense' (p 98). The Egalitarian Fallacy is therefore for Smith simply the bad dream of an objectivism which is unable to imagine a world other than its own; the lack of absolute values no more makes all other values interchangeable than the absence of an agreed gold standard makes all world currencies worth the same.

Smith devotes the last chapter of her *Contingencies of Value* to an energetic defence of relativism against the two principal objections which are usually made against it. The first of these is that it is self-refuting, since, if all truth is relative, then this must be true of the statement about all truth being relative, which must therefore grant its own relativity. As Smith argues, this is really another effect of the inability of objectivist or absolutist thought to conceive any other view of the world but its own. The relativist position, she argues, is not self-refuting, because it is not a logical deduction, or statement of the fundamental truth of things in the objectivist's strong sense. If Smith's kind of relativism 'cannot found, ground, or prove itself, cannot deduce or demonstrate its own rightness' (p 183), in other words, cannot prove itself in principle, then it is equally not susceptible of any refutation in principle. For this reason, if the relativist's view of the world seems to require adjustment or modification, this is not to be taken as evidence of its untruth, in the strong sense. Rather, its self-consistency is demonstrated in the fact that 'it conceives of itself as continuously changing, of all conceptions of the irreducibly various as irreducibly various, and on the multiply configurable as always configurable otherwise' (*ibid*).

The second charge that Smith is concerned to rebut is that, since it discourages commitment to absolute principles and to the programmes of action that are usually founded upon them, relativism encourages at best 'a condition of genial, torpid philosophical que-serà-seràism' and at worst a complete moral paralysis. Her answer to this charge is, firstly, that it places far too much faith in the power of moral absolutism, which has hardly had conspicuous success in keeping away 'the jackals, the Gulag and the death camps' (p 154); but secondly, and more importantly, that it drastically caricatures the nature of the relativist:

> Someone's distaste for or inability to grasp notions such as

'absolute value' and 'objective truth' does not in itself deprive her of such other human characteristics, relevant to moral action, as memory, imagination, early training and example, conditioned loyalties, instinctive sympathies and antipathies, and so forth. Nor does it deprive her of all interest in the subtler, more diffuse, and longer-range consequences of her actions and the actions of others, or oblige her, more than anyone else, to be motivated only by immediate self-interest. (p 161)

The problem with Barbara Herrnstein Smith's account is that while it constitutes a powerful and fiercely precise description from the outside of the conditions and contingencies of value choices, it appears not to be able to theorise the force of value from the inside. Most remarkably, it appears to be unaware of the powerful evaluative force which its own argument exercises and which apparently contradicts elements of that argument. I believe this to be the problem with all such attempts to assert the absolute absence of absolutes.

Strikingly, although she is concerned to demonstrate that relativists are perfectly capable of vigorous evaluative activity, Smith avoids explicitly characterising the value of a relativist view of value. Indeed, she quite emphatically insists that 'given only the denial of objectivism which is sufficient to evoke the quietist objection, *no particular moral positions or types or modes of moral action follow from it at all*, neither those typically attributed to "relativism", such as liberalism, egalitarian tolerance, and passivity, or any others' (p 161). Although her point here is to demonstrate that relativists are not necessarily morally quietistic, her reply to the specimen question 'how would you answer the Nazi?' is rather alarming. As one might expect, she tells us that, like everything else under the moon, *'it depends'* (p 154) – depends, that is on the relative circumstances and dispositions of power between the Nazi and the relativist. What is said to the Nazi, or done in response to the Nazi, depends, in other words, on what pragmatic possibilities present themselves; and, she says, this is in fact what has intended to happen in all cases anyway. But there has been a dramatic narrowing of the force of the question

here, which surely means not only 'how would you be
likely to answer the Nazi?' but also, 'how *should* you answer
the Nazi?' – not, of course, under all or any circumstances,
but in circumstances that did not constrain your evaluative
possibilities. Smith here seems to see no possibility of any
distinction between contingent circumstances and imperatives which transcend them, no possibility that one might
indeed, under some circumstances, say nothing to the
Nazi, and yet regret it profoundly, or judge it to be an
error or failure.

Smith goes on to suggest that anyway we are mistaken in
thinking that answering the Nazi is a matter primarily of
'getting one's ethical/epistemological arguments in good
axiological order', and suggests that what is really required
is 'a theoretically subtle and powerful analysis of the
conditions and, even more important, *dynamics* of the
Nazi's emergence and access to power and, accordingly, a
specification of political and other actions that might make
that emergence and access less likely, both in one's own
neighborhood and elsewhere' (pp 154-5). Here, again, the
question of value has been collapsed into the strategic
question of how to make sense of the contingent factors
that have encouraged and sustained Nazism. The question
of how to describe or interpret Nazism has here replaced
the question of how to evaluate it (in the strong sense,
meaning the question of how, if at all, to justify attempting
to suppress or destroy it). Evaluation has mysteriously
dropped out of Smith's account, or, to be more precise, it
is not exposed to analysis, not itself subject to evaluation.
For there is a form of evaluative assumption present here
– we seek to understand Nazism, she says, in order to
make its emergence in our neighbourhood less likely.
Why, one wants to ask, should one want in the first place to
make Nazism less likely in one's neighbourhood? Smith's
answer, or failure to develop an answer, seems to indicate
that this is not the sort of question a relativist can cope
with, and that we perhaps just have to accept that there
never is a 'first place' any more than a last analysis, and
that the contingencies of 'where the Nazi and I – given, of
course, my particular identity – each are' will determine

entirely whether or not we embrace Nazism.

The principal objection I want to make about this revealing passage of exemplification is not the one that Smith is concerned to defend herself against, namely that this kind of relativism does not allow one to make judgements or evaluations. The problem with this account of relativism is that it makes evaluative choices (usually the choices of others) either seem entirely determined, entirely the product of their contingent circumstances, or (usually when they are one's own acknowledged or unacknowledged values) entirely spontaneous, and beyond the reach of evaluative scrutiny. One of the most serious consequences of this is that Smith's subtle analysis remains alienated from its own powerful evaluative force. For example: objectivist thought, she argues, typically not only accords an absolute value and distinction to what are in fact the contingent values of particular powerful groups, it also operates to devalue the pleasures and values of others. This she calls the 'The-Other's-Poison-Effect', explaining that it means 'not only that one man's meat is another man's poison but that one man sometimes gets sick just *watching* the other fellow eat his meat and, moreover, that if one of them is a cultural theorist (left-wing or conservative as otherwise measured), he or she may be expected to generate an account of how the other fellow is actually being poisoned by the meat he likes and eats' (p 26). This joins with a more generalised sensitivity throughout *Contingencies of Value* to the forms of exclusion and violence practised as a consequence of objectivist notions of absolute value as well as to the 'securing of authority from interrogation and risk' (p 161) that the upholding of absolute standards may seem to bring with it. Against these effects, Smith suggests that 'it might be thought that there was some communal value to ensuring that authority was *always* subject to interrogation and *always* at risk. *All* authority: which must mean that of parent, teacher, and missionary as well as that of tyrant, pope, and state flunky (p 161).

There is a surprising imperative force here ('*all* authority', she insists), even though the reason that Smith offers may seem modest and pragmatic ('it might be thought that there was some communal value' in this). But elsewhere in her argument she is deeply suspicious of the notion that community either in the narrow or large sense could provide ultimate moral justification, and criticises, for example, the residues of teleology and idealism in Richard Rorty's recent arguments that we should prefer solidarity to truth (pp 166-73). However, Smith's suspicion of the values of community leads her, not into moral atomism, a sense of the impossibility of any communitarian horizon in the face of the irreducible diversity and incommensurability of patterns of allegiance, identification and investment, but rather to an articulation of the need, *in the light of* this diversity, for 'the continuous development and refinement of more richly articulated nonobjectivist accounts of, among other things, "truth", "belief", "choice", "justification", and "community"' (p 173). But the scepticism here can never be total, if only because it seems based on a desire not to do violence to the irreducible diversity of human beings and their forms of social organisation and interaction – in other words, based on some form of communal value. The more Smith insists on the requirement not to impose universalist accounts falsely or prematurely, the more commitment she displays to the ideal of an expanded, more richly diversified sense of community. This value appears to be absolute rather than relative, since it is the expression of the principle of the desirability of general improvement. In order to demonstrate that the relativist can indeed make meaningful value-choices, Smith must display her commitment to such general improvement, aimed, not at any form of positive utopia, but rather at the best that can be achieved, that 'general optimum' which consists of 'that set of conditions that permits and encourages, precisely, *evaluation*, and specifically that continuous process described here in relation to both scientific and artistic activity: that is, the local figuring/working out, as well as we, heterogeneously, can, of what seems to work better rather than worse' (p 179).

It is hard to see how one could conceive of, or

recommend the achievement of a 'general optimum' based entirely on case-by-case reasoning, or 'local figuring/ working out', since even this must involve the projection and orientation towards some general moral and evaluative perspective, even if the force of this orientation is expressed in a conscious and vigilant refraining from absolutist intervention in local dispute. For the kind of evaluation that Smith is recommending here is not the simple abandonment or unconsciousness of the horizon of absolute value, but rather a knowledgeable, sensitive and principled holding off from the violence of objectivism, educated by her own richly-diversified, and therefore powerfully inclusive account of value.

The commitment to the achievement of a general optimum implies a commitment to another form of non-negotiable value. For, we might want to ask, why should 'we', heterogeneously or not (and it is hard to imagine what a completely heterogeneous 'we' could possibly be) bother? Why not actually recommend conflict, tyranny, or degeneration, rather than the encouraging prospects set out here? It may be replied, because these things are less desirable to most people, and it is not only more sensible, but also better to go for what seems better rather than worse. Surely one noncontingent value is being asserted here, even if it is of a rather abstract kind, namely, the value of evaluative choice and action, in fact, the irreducible value of value itself.

There seems, for example, to be no possibility of admitting the contingency of her own view of the contingency of all value. Between contingency and absolutism, as she emphasises at many points through *Contingencies of Value*, there can only be stand-off, with no possibility of negotiation, or 'local figuring/working out'. For the most part, Smith presents this as the fault of the absolutist, who refuses to believe in the possibility of value aside from absolute value and therefore can only caricature the relativist case. For an absolutist to understand the claims of a relativist, she would have already to have abandoned absolutism. But the intractabi- lity works in the other direction, too. For the relativist, there is no possibility of accommodation with absolutist thought. Absolutism must be absolutely rejected, since the idea of a limited or partial absolutism is, of course, ludicrous. To be fair, Smith does try at one point to demonstrate such a partial adjustment to absolutism, when she suggests that 'it would be no more logically inconsistent for a nonobjectivist to speak, under *some* conditions, of fundamental rights and objective facts than for a Hungarian ordering his lunch in Paris to speak French' (p 158). But the flexible relativist could not be said here to be really speaking of fundamental truths and objective facts, except as a kind of strategy or imposture. Of course, Smith's remark here might be interpreted as meaning that all fundamentalist and objectivist thought is really strategic in this manner, whether consciously or not, but this demonstrates, not the mutual accommodation of relativism and absolutism, but, again, the triumph of the relativist case. Once again, we arrive at an impasse, in the 'game of pure nonengagement, ending in a draw by default' (p 156).

Smith argues that this very impasse, or the perception of it as an impasse, is further evidence of the inflexibility of the objectivist, since 'The idea that conceptualizations are radically contingent, and that conceptual/discursive impasses may be intractable will be, to the objectivist, a mark of relativism' (p 156). But is not such a situation also 'a mark of relativism' for the relativist and, in some sense a demonstration of the preferability of a relativist case to an absolutist one? And is this not a mirror-image of the absolutists' aggressive annexation to the terms of their worldview of everything that opposes it? The absolutist says, 'the fact that we cannot agree is proof of the chaos that results from abandoning faith in absolutes', while the relativist says 'the fact that we cannot agree is proof of the untenability of absolutist positions', each side proving its case by its interpretation of the terms of the disagreement. The impasse results, in other words, from the intractability of both sides of the argument, not just from the absolutist's refusal to understand the point of view of the relativist. There seems no way for the relativist to tolerate absolutism as a mere difference of conceptual style or philosophical idiom, since this very toleration is lethal to the absolutist case. The situation is nicely illustrated by the joke about the new arrival in Heaven who is shown the adherents of the various denominations and religions of the world enjoying their posthumous bliss; noticing the absence of any Catholics, the arrival is told by St Peter that they have to be kept in a separate compartment since, as St Peter explains, 'they think they're the only ones here'. It is a joke that can be told to the discredit of any absolutist creed, since its point is to show that the toleration of an absolutism is in fact its intellectual confounding.

My point here is that, in all these respects, in its unswerving commitment to the notion of general betterment, the collective value of value, and its absolute commitment to the contingency of all absolutes, Barbara Herrnstein's account is paradoxical and deficient. It may appear that my objection is really only a version of the classical argument of self-refutation which is often directed against relativism, and which Smith claims can be answered by the counter-argument that relativism does not make truth-claims that are strong enough to make it vulnerable to self-refutation. But I am not concerned to argue here that Smith's relativism refutes itself, or that her argument is deficient *because* it is paradoxical. Its deficiency lies not in any failure to expunge paradox or self-contradiction, but in its failure to recognise its own paradoxical structure (indeed the paradoxical structure of all value-systems), and to seek to articulate and explore it.

I believe that it would be possible to show in a similar way that any of the current relativisms or alleged relativisms in fact rely upon certain values that are not held to be relative. The point of doing so, however, would not be to re-establish the authority of the absolutist case, in the quasi-Kantian 'critique of pure value' suggested by Kate Soper which is designed 'to acquire a better sense of the minimal value-commitments essential to the critical power of social and cultural theory'.[8] The point is not to reassert any kind of bottom line of value, but rather to demonstrate that there is really no absolute choice possible between the retrieval and critique of values, minimal or otherwise: no choice possible between absolutism and relativism, between transcendent and contingent values, between essences and history. For it is impossible to choose plurality without making an absolute commitment to the absolute desirability of plurality; just as it is impossible to imagine any absolute value – absolute beauty, universal freedom, equality, justice – which would not have in principle to be vulnerable to the kind of relativising critique with which the last couple of decades have made us familiar.

The question of value cannot be seized all at once or all together, and this precisely because absolute value and relative value are not the sundered halves of a totality. Rather, each follows from and is implied within the other. Even to acknowledge this paradoxical structure of value, necessary and important though it is, is not to make the question of value knowable or masterable as a whole or entire structure. If this is very far from the assertion of the possibility of fixed values, then neither is it anything as simple as an assertion of 'play' or pure relativity against such fixity; rather, it is to suggest that what seems to us like fixity is coiled closely together with what seems like play. These peculiar torsions in the question of value make a strange, continuous kind of claim upon us, for we can never be entirely separate from the question of value, never fully escape its gravitational pull, nor ever fully inhabit it as our home, or *ethos*. The question of value will always exert an imperative force which disturbs us from our safe inhabitation of ourselves, impelling us to question beliefs, certainties and values, with a view, not only to their potential betterment, but to the revaluation of the very notions of better and worse. The necessity of value is thus endlessly to value and revalue our values themselves. But it is absurd to think of this imperative as coming from outside our selves, even if its force is to evict us from our complacent tenure of the first person plural. The paradoxical structure of value, in its immanent transcendence, is what enables and requires us to recognise that it is only in the absolute putting of the 'we' at risk that we realise the possibilities of our humanity. Neither side of this paradox, the side of risk or the side of realisation, is definitive, or can diminish the necessity of the other.

Notes

1 'Introductory Notes for a Postmodern Value Agenda', in *Life After Postmodernism: Essays on Value and Culture*, John Fekete, (ed.) Macmillan, London 1988, p i.

2 *Contingencies of Value: Alternative Perspectives for Critical Theory*, Harvard University Press, Cambridge, Mass. and London, 1988), pp 17-18. References will be given hereafter in the text.

3 *The Political Unconscious: Narrative as a Socially Symbolic Act*, Methuen, London and New York, 1981, p 59.

4 Two important carriers of the critique of aesthetic ideology are, Pierre Bourdieu, whose *Distinction: A Social Critique of the Judgement of Taste* (trans. Richard Nice, Routledge and Kegan Paul, London and New York, 1984) urges a reintegration of the aesthetic and sociopolitical with a reading of the social and cultural capital constituted by cultural and aesthetic competence: and Terry Eagleton, whose *The Ideology of the Aesthetic* Basil Blackwell (Cambridge, Mass. and Oxford 1990) sees the category of the aesthetic as a means simultaneously to displace and consolidate relations of political power.

5 John Dewey, *Theory of Valuation, The Later Works, 1925-1953*, Jo Ann Boyditon and Barbara Levine, (eds), Southern Illinois University Press, Carbondale and Edwardsville, 1988, Vol. 13, p 195.

6 Jean-François Lyotard and Jean-Loup Thébaud, *Just Gaming*, trans. Brian Massumi, Manchester University Press, Manchester, 1985, pp 66, 67.

7 Kate Soper, this collection, p 19.

8 Ibid., p 28.

An Answer to Relativism?

PAUL HIRST

Does relativism matter? This may seem an odd question, since intense debate between the several varieties of objectivism and the several varieties of relativism is a prominent feature of the contemporary intellectual scene. Many conservative objectivists see the pervasive relativism in the academy and modern culture as a threat to civilization itself. Writers like Derrida and Foucault are seen as a pan-disciplinary plague, sweeping into disciplines like literary studies, philosophy, and sociology, but also into unexpected areas like accountancy, architecture, and law. A critic like Allan Bloom in *The Closing of the American Mind*, for example, sees the relativistic attitudes of teachers in the humanities as a threat not only to scholarship but to fundamental cultural values.[1]

On the other side of the fence many radical intellectuals have embraced what they see as the fundamental pluralism and relativism of 'postmodernism'. The postmodern condition is one in which intellectual work is no longer constrained by prescriptive and scientistic methodologies or dragooned by totalising discourses that seek to prescribe a necessary future and a 'progressive' social role for the intellectual. The free play of discourse, the breaking-down of the boundaries between criticism and creativity, between the pretensions to a purely logical discourse and writing, are the gains of postmodernity. It is those committed to an Enlightenment conception of knowledge as emancipatory truth or to the positivist vision of science as value-neutral objective research who are trying to sustain an obsolete myth of the role of the intellectual. It is a myth that can avoid putting knowledge at the service of domination only by the intellectually tyrannical device of imagining a necessary future and the essential role of knowledge in bringing about that future and 'setting us free'.

Conservative objectivists and radical postmodernists both link their discussions of the place of the intellectual to epistemological questions. I shall argue that whilst linking the two sets of questions is necessary, their ways of doing so are unhelpful in mitigating the consequences of relativism. Both sides in the debate tend to overblow the contest into a battle for the future of civilization.

Like most debates in which the 'future of civilization' has apparently been at stake, nothing much actually happens. Civilization doesn't end. It needs more than squabbling intellectuals to bring that about. Most disciplines can survive a superstructure of methodological and meta-theoretical debate. It is only in knowledges and disciplinary areas that are in grave trouble anyway that interminable and corrosive methodological struggles break out and come to inhibit other activities. The other reason nothing much happens is that most of the 'debates' are inextricably confused. Imaginary enemies are created and then defeated; the complex varieties of relativism get lumped together and attacked and then defended in turn as if they represented a homogeneous 'problem'. Most relativists are not stupid enough to believe the positions ascribed to them, and most 'refutations' of relativism are so meretricious that intelligent people who have other reasons for saying what they do simply carry on regardless. Few disciplines are strongly enough controlled by explicit methodological protocols for a methodological debate to be decisive in its effect on their activities. Most disciplines have largely unexamined presuppositions or founding myths that make rational conformity to a methodological programme impossible, particularly to one imported from outside.

Many knowledges' general doctrines are in practice

curious amalgams of universalistic and relativistic, objectivist and conventionalist arguments. Only in the field of pure epistemology and general methodological doctrines can clear, abstract positions be taken on one side or the other of the relativist and objectivist divide. But then such positions are uncontaminated by and therefore also less effective on the messy necessities of intellectual work. Social antropology is a good example of this complex crossing of relativist and non-relativist arguments in a definite discipline. A certain relativism is virtually constitutive of modern social anthropology. Anthropology exists by virtue of cultural difference, radical divergences in cultural values and social ways of living. It explores those differences as the product of social relations and socially conditioned beliefs. It is compelled to consider socially and culturally specific beliefs, values, and knowledges as consequential for social activities. It follows that, considered from the standpoint of social relations, certain activities are socially necessary and a sufficient degree of conformity to them is a condition for the continuance of the social order. Anthropology is condemned to see both sides of the Pyrenees as living by codes appropriate to their conditions. If it does not, it gradually shades into some other discipline or activity, one which acts to reduce difference according to a general programme of its own rather than to reflect it.

But anthropologists are not constitutively committed to a methodological relativism that reduces knowledge to a mere perspectivalism. Some radical relativists do argue that cultural difference is not merely an object of knowledge but necessarily enters into knowledge itself. Societies can be known only in terms of their own meanings and these meanings are incommensurable with our own and cannot be fully translated into our own language. Such a view explodes anthropology as a social science; instead it becomes a series of mutually incompatible and socially conditioned societal perspectives. It is ultimately destructive of anthropology itself, since by denying any comparability or generalisability of anthropological knowledge, it makes difference absolute and incommunicable. But anthropologists opposed to this perspectivalism are not thereby committed to some particular objectivist epistemological doctrine or to a strong form of universalism in which anthropology is seen as part of a unified scientific enterprise using one set of common methodological protocols. To refuse the consequences of one position does not necessarily imply embracing its mirror opposite.

The Pre-Modern Condition

Anthropology is not alone in being constituted by a certain type of relativism. The Jesuit missionaries of the seventeenth century recognized the necessity of accepting, understanding, and adapting to cultural difference. God had created a world where the institutions sustaining Christendom were confined to certain localities. The Christian message was, however, universal and Christians must preach it to all. How then to deal with stable, well-governed pagan societies like Japan and China whose civilized elites had developed their own codes of ethics and beliefs? In order to carry the Christian message elsewhere its envoys had to adapt it to other beliefs, other institutions, and other expectations, to render it intelligible and acceptable. This led to the subversive conclusion that God's message had itself been adapted to its first receptors and that the Bible was an amalgam of eternal truths and an expository content adapted to the people to whom they were revealed.[2] In like manner the different classes and conditions of persons in Christian society needed a message and a set of religious practices adapted to their different circumstances. Haughty but delicate aristocratic ladies needed quite different penances from peasants, for example. Jesuit casuistry, sophisticated in its relativism and complex in its application to different conditions, repelled many of the more fundamentally and puristically pious. Pascal's *Provincial Letters* are a devastating criticism of Jesuit casuistry, but founded on a pious incomprehension of the necessities driving the Jesuits towards such a practice.[3]

This reference to the Jesuits should remind us that the fear of relativism is nothing new. Relativism usually springs from a set of differences that cannot be eliminated by argument or evidence alone. Such differences are not merely intellectual, they include not only quite distinct forms of or approaches to knowledge, but different patterns of social beliefs and different institutions. Relativism of a non-meretricious kind usually stems from the recognition of such difference as inescapable, or, where relativism is conceived as a form of pluralism, as actually beneficial. Anti-relativism, on the contrary, often stems from a commitment to one of the different forms in contest and at worst leads to a wish to eliminate the others.

The modern world is not the first to experience radical difference in knowledge, belief, and institutions as both a fact and, for some, a problem. People who regard the 'postmodern condition' as unique generally seem to believe the world began in 1900. Well, it did not, and laments about a world in which radically incompatible ideas, beliefs, and institutions exist are not new. Late antiquity involved a fundamental conflict between a highly developed but narrowly elitist pagan high culture and Christianity, a conflict reflected graphically in Augustine's *Confessions*.[4] Again, the seventeenth century presented a problem to sophisticated Christian intellectuals: the problem of an absent God (*deus absconditus*). God had revealed His message to man in the Bible, but He no longer spoke directly to man. How then to divine His purposes and reach Him in a world of conflicting religious doctrines and radically different beliefs about His motives and purposes? This was a problem as tormenting to Catholics like Pascal as to Calvinists like Pierre Bayle. Uncertainty was created, not merely by the fact of religious difference but by the impact of philosophical scepticism on both sides of the religious divide. Pascal offered a thoroughly 'modern' solution in the form of his 'wager'. The essence of Pascal's dilemma: uncertainty and sceptical belief lead to eternal damnation if God exists, whilst belief leads to eternal felicity. Even if the probability that God exists is small, the costs of not wagering that He does exist are incalculable if we do at last come before Him. Belief is thus a rational decision even in a situation of extreme doubt and uncertainty.

Pascal was trying to rescue faith from uncertainty, from the corrosive effects of a plurality of religious systems, but by intellectual means far removed from the certainties of traditional faith.[5] Bayle, unlike Pascal, does not seek to overcome scepticism but rather to use it to explore and explode the confusions created by religious doctrines for religious belief itself. Bayle showed, for example, the impossibility of arriving at a satisfactory theodicy and of resolving the problem of evil by means of reason. Faith could be found only by individuals. Therefore, all forced conversion to religious doctrine as a way of resolving religious differences was not merely unjust but ineffective. Bayle produced the best and most thoroughgoing arguments for religious toleration of his time. Religious toleration and the insistence, on religious grounds, of freedom of individual conscience in matters of religion, offered a way out of the impasse of contesting religious dogmas. A plurality of doctrines each claiming to be the true faith and each in bitter contest to extirpate the others could only ruin religion.[6]

The difference between the seventeenth century and today is not that of a plurality of incompatible views, but rather that our incompatible views are about quite different things, such as economic policy or lifestyle politics, and that where differences about religion remain they are in an entirely new context. Modern intellectuals are even more confused than were seventeenth-century thinkers like Bayle. We are no longer predominantly concerned with the question of which is the true faith. Modern intellectuals are far more diverse in aims, methods, and social positions than were the theologians representing the contesting Christian confessions in the seventeenth century. However, what turning to the example of thinkers like Pascal and Bayle shows is that often the most effective way of coping with radical differences in ideas is to side-step them. Pascal's 'wager' and Bayle's use of scepticism to reveal the impossibility of arriving at a consistent religious doctrine, and, therefore, the unjustifiability of compelling observance of such doctrine, are precisely such strategies for overcoming conflicts.

A plurality of religious beliefs mattered in the seventeenth century because religion remained the predominant human concern. Today the situation is more complicated. We have multiple domains in which there are pluralities of view, and it is difficult either to rank or to separate them. Indeed, these distinct domains are often aggregated by people who think the world is going to pot because we do not stick to the old verities. But what are the old verities and do they in turn hang together? Why should we aggregate together people who subscribe to Paul Feyerabend's relativistic anti-methodology[7] and people who believe in multicultural education? Presumably one can be an unreconstructed Popperian and yet believe in multicultural education – it may even count as 'piecemeal social engineering'? Curious amalgams are built up on both sides of this 'debate'. 'Western' values, objective scientific truth, and the institution of the 'bourgeois' family add up to a consistent whole to some, and are seen as threatened by subversive 'relativist' arguments. The assumption here is that we can reconstruct a homogeneous cultural and social world – an assumption which, moreover, makes it possible to be simultaneously and connectedly worried about epistemological doctrines and whether gay activists have too much influence on children.

Competing Methodologies and the Disciplinary Field

If one chooses to remain at the level of abstract epistemological doctrines the battle-lines between relativism and objectivism are clear, but the underlying sources of the conflict are less intelligible. For example, many people have subscribed to Thomas Kuhn's views in *The Structure of Scientific Revolutions* about incommensurable paradigms and scientific change through revolution[8] for reasons that have little to do with its merits as an account of the history of science and a great deal to do with their generally radical political views or with the internal politics in their own discipline. Epistemological conflicts are so often a displaced forum for other differences. If anything it is fields that are radically unlike the major natural sciences – sociology, for example – that are most influenced by methodologies derived from the philosophy of science.

Prescriptive and objectivist epistemological doctrines are effective only in so far as they inhibit what can be said or done in a particular disciplinary field, by imposing a single model of what knowledge should look like. In so far as that model is in conflict with the objectives and actual working methods of members of the discipline these members will resist it in various ways, including producing relativist or conventionalist arguments to counter the legislative pretensions of the epistemological doctrine in question. Relativism is thus in part a by-product of objectivism and universalism imposed in the form of prescriptive methodological protocols. Epistemological arguments are inherently indecisive precisely because generalised methodological doctrines cannot actually 'guarantee' standards of validity or procedures of research in particular fields. These standards and procedures have to be developed at a quite different level and may have little connection in practice with the prevailing doctrine of which they are supposed to be exemplars.

Likewise relativistic arguments, even if they deny the relevance of prescriptive epistemological doctrines, are effective only in terms of their impact on a particular disciplinary field. This impact can be beneficial if it preserves the autonomy of work in a certain area, or detrimental if it undermines research by problematicising its status. Many Marxists in the west opposed Popperian and logical postivist models of knowledge based on the natural sciences precisely because they saw them as means of relegating Marxism to the junk-heap category of unverifiable or unfalsifiable metaphysics. Often they did so by means of relativistic arguments and by conceiving Marxism as a humanistic intellectual activity quite distinct from the supposed positivism of the natural sciences. This has also been the tactic of sociologists seeking to avoid the model of valid knowledge as the discovery of general laws.

An example of a disastrous form of relativism is to be found in the sociology of deviance. The tactic here is to demonstrate that as standards of conduct differ between societies and different historical periods in the same society, the currently prevailing conceptions of crime, delinquency, mental illness, etc, are merely 'normative expressions' of our society and lack objectivity. As a tactic in questioning uncritical positivists in criminology or medicine, who identify their own actions with objectivity, this has at best limited value. It becomes absurd when one moves beyond such criticism to ask 'What then *should* one do?' We are not helped greatly by being told that things were done differently in medieval Europe or that quite different conceptions prevail among the Hopi, and that our ways of doing things are historically limited and not inevitable. True, but we are trying to deal with certain problems of conduct and are not living in a perpetual sociology seminar. As the relativism of anthropology indicates, certain beliefs and activities are necessary to certain social relations. The sociologist cannot pretend to be an indifferent observer or a merely clever academic critic of his or her society for ever, without paying the price of being seen as such and dismissed as an irrelevancy.[9]

Politics and Knowledge in a Pluralist Era

Relativist arguments *can* be intellectually destructive but so can the use of objectivist epistemological doctrines as part of an intellectual 'police action', putting certain theories, methods of working, and objects of knowledge in the category of the impermissible. The problem is that despite this we *do* need to differentiate between valid and invalid theories, knowledge, and ideas. And not only in the academy. A world in which 'anything goes' might be all right so long as all participants accepted that that was so; one would have to tolerate things one felt were silly but at least one would be tolerated in turn.[10] But some participants in such a world would abuse the liberty of 'anything goes' to impose their own views, certain of which would be simply intolerable: for example, the parading of race prejudice as if it were objective scientific knowledge. In such a relativist Utopia creationists would enjoy *de facto* equal regard with evolutionary biology in educational establishments.

We cannot abandon the search for specific standards of validity as if they were no more than an old-fashioned nineteenth-century positivist illusion, out of date in a world of multiple perspective and the creative use of whatever discursive resources we please. Validity – the determination of whether a belief or a knowledge claim is justified or not – in an issue that predated modern science, nineteenth-century positivism, and the Enlightenment. As we have seen, in the seventeenth century the issue of the validity of forms of *faith* was a central question. In the seventeenth century this issue of the validity of faith was the burning question of knowledge: far more important than the validity of propositions about the natural world. Today the political sustainability of beliefs in a pluralist era is far more central to the issue of relativism and validity than any purely methodological dispute about academic disciplines.

Validity is as much a political issue as it is an intellectual one. What beliefs are taken as valid determines the whole tenor of the social order. Some beliefs may be legally tolerable as private eccentricities. I can believe the earth is flat; but this belief would be deleterious if I should become a successful educational reformer seeking to give this view equal time with other views in schools. Certain beliefs have not merely to be struggled against intellectually, to be shown to be wrong, but also legally proscribed in order to prevent them from having social effect. If it is objected that this is illiberal, the answer is that certain beliefs *are* wrong and that their propagation has had or could have disastrous consequences, as the example of scientific racism demonstrates. To claim to be justified in legally proscribing the active advocacy of race supremacy, we must, however, feel justified in the belief that scientific racism is not valid.

Any society sets limits to beliefs. In societies where there is the presumption of freedom of opinion and toleration of different views, the suppression of belief needs to be based on more than an opposing belief, on righteous prejudice. It must be based on the justifiable claim that the belief subject to challenge is unjustifiable, invalid, and harmful. Liberal societies have to be pluralistic and relativistic, but within limits. If they concede that 'anything goes' in the matter of opinion and that one person's validity is another person's trash, and so be it, then they are in danger of dissolution.

A liberal polity has to keep well away from righteous prejudice, but it cannot evade the question of the validity of its members' beliefs and the consequences arising therefrom. It will not be greatly helped in this by philosophical epistemology or methodological doctrines developed in the philosophy of science. To this an objection may be raised: 'How then *is* the validity or invalidity of a belief to be assessed?' The answer is simple, by arguing and showing it to be valid or otherwise. This task has always to be accomplished by arguments and evidence appropriate to the specific case in question. If these demonstrations or demolitions work, they work; there are no general 'guarantees' other than the specific processes of arguing and showing that will make them work. To ask 'How do we know that our arguments are valid, our evidence is sufficient?' is to pitch us back into the domain of 'guarantees' and into the morass of philosophical epistemology. We can answer the question only by hammering out the arguments and amassing the evidence.

But surely people can agree to be convinced by bad arguments and unsatisfactory evidence? Yes, they do so all the time, often in pursuit of conformity with methodological protocols. Consensus is usually the product of forces other than methodological argument and usually reflects a wider consensus with other determinants. What if we are convinced in matters of validity merely as a matter of convenient consensus, if all we have is an agreement to agree that x or y is or is not the case? Such agreements to agree are not a general problem; they can be a specific problem but they can also be part and parcel of a sustainable intellectual and social order. Some agreements to agree are inescapable, even if they rest on social consensus rather than quality of argument, on the acceptance of the validity of certain beliefs determined by unexamined presuppositions and myths. All disciplines and societies have some elements of such agreements to agree as a constitutive part of their activities. If they become self-defeating, if irreconcilable differences arise, then arguments about validity break out. We may be victims of our own assumptions about method and the entities that exist in our world but we can never be wholly free of such assumptions. This is one of the greatest illusions of legislative epistemology, that we can ground by pure philosophy how we know that we know without error, illusion and compromise.

Indeed, one can say that the worst sort of agreements to agree are not those that arise from unargued presuppositions but, on the contrary, those that would arise from the conviction that we possess general and satisfactory methodological protocols. If one thinks a particular epistemological doctrine is a sovereign remedy against methodological error then one is in grave danger of such a dangerous consensus breaking out. In fact the general acceptance of such a doctrine could itself be the product of an agreement to agree, which would then determine in a general way what are to count as good and bad arguments. How then would we verify those claims? We could not; we would be the victims of our own invincible methodological ignorance.

Actually, this form of invincible ignorance has seldom been stabilised for long. We do not have one dominant epistemological doctrine but a plurality of doctrines, each of which jostles the others for priority and each of which provides counter-defences against the presumptions and partialities of the others. Methodological pluralism is a fact of life. It also provides resources for a mutual check on the pretensions as to standards of validity that each epistemological doctrine necessarily shares.

Usually, this methodological pluralism enters into contests about standards of good and bad argument only by providing general 'philosophical cover': arguments about validity are actually conducted at a less general level and hinge on specific issues and focuses of dispute. Trying to establish the validity of beliefs by specific processes of arguing and showing is no guarantee against falsehood. But endlessly posing the general question 'How do you know that you know?' and seeking a general philosophical answer is no guarantee either. Arguing and showing are, of course, single words for a multiplicity of styles of reasoning and forms of evidentialisation.[11] The form of argument or the type of evidence used will depend on the case at issue, the discipline in question, and the broader social and political implications of the validity of the ideas or beliefs in question. The fact that reason is not all of a piece, that styles of argument and standards of evidence change over time and with reference to the issues involved is not a general problem. To try to make it so is to enter into the same kind of relativistic limbo as the sociologists of deviance mentioned above. That is to say, the challenge to the styles and standards we currently use that they are historically and socially specific is no challenge at all.

That styles of reasoning and standards of evidence change does not undo, of itself, the arguing and showing of either the past or the present. The determination of the validity of belief by methods that we no longer use was effective in its time for the purposes of its time. We think none the worse of past refutations of erroneous beliefs because they were accomplished with the aid of methods of reasoning we would not employ today. Equally, we are not threatened by the fact that past thinkers we deem valuable and intelligent contributors to our present state of knowledge were led by their general styles of argument to conclusions we know to be erroneous. Leading thinkers of the sixteenth and seventeenth centuries argued rigorously for the existence of witches or the legal validity of persecuting people accused of being such. We do not believe in witches and feel secure in our grounds for knowing belief in the reality and efficacy of witchcraft to be false. We can appreciate why thinkers argued as they did from their premisses and why they made the assumptions they did. We can see these premisses and assumptions to be wrong, but we can appreciate the rigour and efficacy of their arguments in the context of such premisses and assumptions. Some of our own ideas and arguments will doubtless fall into the same category. This fact does not, however, undermine any of our specific arguments or processes of evidentialisation: only counter-arguments and counter-evidence effective in the present can do that.[12]

A degree of epistemological and ethical relativism is inescapable today. We live in a world with an increasing multiplicity of different disciplines and types of knowledge. We would be more than hard-pressed to find a single methodological doctrine that adequately covered and respected this diversity and yet which was not impossibly bland as a result of doing so. We live in a world of differing ethical standards and social objectives, in which a certain social pluralism is the only answer to either perpetual strife or the tyrannical imposition of one set of values. At both levels a degree of acceptance of diversity by a species of relativism is necessary. It is a condition for a degree of toleration. But a generalised relativism that dodges the issue of the validity of beliefs in a complete epistemological and social liberalism is a dangerous accentuation of the differences we encounter. We also face the necessity of imposing justified limits on belief in both the intellectual and the social spheres if the world of knowledge and society as a whole is not to be torn apart by the consequences of certain beliefs.

I have tried to avoid discussing the question of relativism at the level of abstract philosophical doctrines *pro* and *contra*. Approaching the question by looking at the social sources of difference which lead to their reflection in relativist views enables us to understand why relativism is endemic and ineradicable in modern intellectual debate. It also enables us to understand why a philosophically generalised and thoroughgoing relativism is incompatible with sustaining the conditions for a tolerant and pluralistic intellectual and political order. This is exactly the opposite conclusion to the one that leading philosophical relativists draw when they argue that freedoms to develop knowledge and political freedom depend on accepting the slogan 'anything goes'. It is also a very different conclusion from those who get hottest under the collar about 'objectivity'. The more grandiloquent forms of objectivism and universalism seek to answer relativism by extirpating it. They perceive it to be a dangerous pest of a single species. In fact such arguments tend to feed the case made by the more generalising relativists about the tyrannical nature of objectivist philosophical doctrines. It is, therefore, easier to argue for the more radical forms of relativism than it otherwise would be and easier to present the issue as if it were a general philosophical one. The objectivist argument simply fails to recognise species of relativism that are not pests, because in order to exist itself it cannot accept that there are such. It thus simply fails to apprehend the forms of relativism which are necessary and constructive in certain disciplines like social anthropology, or the forms of intellectual relativism necessary to the limited pluralism of a sustainable liberal order.

Notes

[1] Allan Bloom, *The Closing of the American Mind*, Simon & Schuster, New York, 1987.

[2] The contact of Christian Europe with hitherto unknown civilizations with radically different cultures is interestingly discussed in Tzvetan Todorov, *The Conquest of the Americas*, Harper & Row, New York, 1984, and in Anthony Pagden, *The Fall of Natural Man*, Cambridge University Press, Cambridge, 1982. On the Jesuits in China see J.D. Spence, *The Memory Palace of Matteo Ricci*, Faber, London, 1985.

[3] See Blaise Pascal, *Pensées*, trans. A.J. Krailsheimer, Penguin, Harmondsworth, 1967. Casuistry is considered by Benjamin Nelson in a number of papers in his collection *On the Roads to Modernity*, T.E. Huff (ed), Rowman & Littlefield, Totowa, NJ, 1981, and in E. Leites (ed), *Conscience and Casuistry in Early Modern Europe*, Cambridge University Press, Cambridge, 1988.

[4] The issue of the conflict between paganism and Christianity is considered by E.R. Dodds in *Pagan and Christian in an Age of Anxiety*, Norton, New York, 1970, and by Arnoldo Momigliano (ed) in *The*

Conflict between Paganism and Christianity in the Fourth Century, Clarendon Press, Oxford, 1963, and St Augustine's early experiences of the conflict of cultures before his full Christian conversion – see his *Confessions*, trans. R.S. Pine-Coffin, Penguin, Harmondsworth, 1961 – are considered in Peter Brown's *Augustine of Hippo*, Faber, London, 1969.

[5] Pascal's 'wager' is to be found in his *Pensées* (*op cit*, passage 418). The wager as a decision procedure is discussed in a fascinating essay by Mary Douglas, 'The social preconditions of radical scepticism', in J. Law (ed), *Power, Action and Belief*, Routledge, London, 1986, in the context of a general discussions of relativism. Ian Hacking in *The Emergence of Probability*, Cambridge University Press, Cambridge, 1975, considers Pascal's wager in the context of the development of probability theory (see especially chapter 8). Hacking also contends that the Jesuit doctrine of probabilism (central to their practice of casuistry) was an intellectual obstacle to the development of modern concepts of probability. The social background to Pascal's religious views is considered in Lucien Goldmann, *The Hidden God*, Routledge, London, 1964, part 3.

[6] For a taste of Bayle's work consult the selected edition of the *Historical and Critical Dictionary*, R.H. Popkin (ed), Bobbs-Merrill, Indianapolis, Ind., 1965. For a valuable short introduction to Bayle's work see Elizabeth Labrousse, *Pierre Bayle*, Oxford Past Masters series, Oxford University Press, Oxford, 1983. On the development of religious toleration see Henry Kamen, *The Rise of Toleration*, Weidenfeld & Nicolson, London, 1967 and on scepticism on this period see R.H. Popkin, *The History of Scepticism from Erasmus to Descartes*, 2nd edn, Harper & Row, New York, 1968.

[7] Paul Feyerabend, *Against Method*, New Left Books, London, 1975.

[8] Thomas Kuhn, *The Structure of Scientific Revolutions*, 2nd edn, University of Chicago Press, Chicago, 1970.

[9] A good example of such sociological relativism is to be found in T.J. Scheff, *Being Mentally Ill*, Aldine, Chicago, 1966. I have discussed this type of sociological relativism further in Paul Hirst and Penny Woolley, *Social Relations and Human Attributes*, Tavistock, London, 1982.

[10] 'Anything goes' is, of course, a well-known slogan from Paul Feyerabend, who with extreme honesty subtitled his *Against Method*, 'Outline of an anarchistic theory of knowledge'. Feyerabend's stricture against the legislative excesses of prescriptive methodology is well taken but to my mind he simply ignores the political implications of 'anything goes' in the realm of knowledge and belief. He consistently seems to suppose that a democracy can avoid legislating in matters of belief.

[11] For the concept of 'styles of reasoning' and a discussion of the implications of the fact that they change, see Ian Hacking, 'Language, truth and reason', in M. Hollis and S. Lukes (eds), *Relativity and Relativism*, Blackwell, Oxford, 1982.

[12] I have discussed this issue of the use of rational arguments to sustain witchcraft belief and the problematicity of explanations of why

persecutions of witches declined at the end of the seventeenth century in Paul Hirst, 'Is it rational to reject relativism', in J. Overing (ed), *Reason and Morality*, Tavistock, London, 1985.

Pluralism and the Politics of Difference

Liberal Socialism and Pluralism: Which Citizenship?

CHANTAL MOUFFE

Pluralism is currently one of those values to which everybody refers but those meaning is unclear and far from being adequately theorised. This absence of a satisfactory theory of pluralism has serious negative consequences for our undersanding of democratic politics. Whilst the current recognition of the virtues of pluralist democracy is an important achievement, to accept 'actually existing capitalist liberal democracies' as the 'end of history' would be a serious setback to the fight for democracy. There are still numerous social relations where the process of democratisation is needed, and the task for the Left today is to envisage how this can be done in a way which is compatible with the existence of a liberal democratic regime. This requires that we scrutinize the relationship that exists between pluralism and individualism and its consequences for citizenship. In *Hegemony and Socialist Strategy*[1] we attempted to redefine the socialist project in terms of 'radical and plural democracy', and to visualise it as the extension of democracy to a wide range of social relations. Our intention was to reinscribe socialist goals within the framework of a pluralist democracy and to insist on the necessity of their articulation with the institutions of political liberalism. Since then, with the collapse of communism, our thesis has been vindicated because it has become evident that socialism can only have a future if it is envisaged as a deepening of the pluralist conquests made by liberal democracy, in other words it must become 'liberal socialism'. In this article I want to examine some of the theoretical problems that arise from the attempt to integrate elements of liberalism and socialism. I argue that it is in the concept of individualism that the main limitation of the liberal approach lies, and here that the socialist tradition of thought could make an important contribution. I will argue that if we want to defend and deepen the pluralism that constitutes the crucial value that liberalism brought to modern democracy, we have to break away from the straitjacket of individualism in order to be able to envisage our identities as citizens in a new way.

Norberto Bobbio and Liberal Socialism

Among socialists, Norberto Bobbio is one of the most eloquent advocates of the need to recognise the value of liberal institutions and to defend them against the critics of 'true democracy'. He has also stated that individualism is constitutive both of liberalism and of democracy. Hence the importance of coming to terms with his arguments. Bobbio has for a long time put forward the thesis not only that socialist goals *could* be realised within the framework of liberal democracy, but that they could *only* be realised acceptably within such a framework. For him, far from being contradictory, liberalism and democracy necessarily go together, and a democratic socialism is thus bound to be a liberal one. He writes 'the liberal state is not only the historical but the legal premise of the democratic state. The liberal state and the democratic state are doubly interdependent: if liberalism provides those liberties necessary to the proper exercise of democratic power, democracy guarantees the existence and persistence of fundamental liberties'.[2]

Bobbio belongs to an important tradition of Italian liberal thought which has since the nineteenth century, under the influence of John Stuart Mill, been receptive to socialist ideas. In the twentieth century this tradition

crystallised around the journal *La Rivoluzione Liberale*
(created by Piero Gobetti), and the movement 'Giustizia e
Liberta' (founded by Carlo Rosselli, author of *Socialismo
Liberale* which argued that socialism must achieve its goals
by the liberal method, within the institutional framework of
liberal democracy.[3]) Their aim was to combine socialist
objectives with the principles of liberal democracy: consti-
tutionalism, parliamentarism and a competitive multi-party
system.

Bobbio is following in this tradition when he argues that
today such a project requires a new social contract that
articulates social justice with civil rights. According to him,
the current debate around contractarianism should provide the terrain for the democratic left to make an
important intervention. He considers that 'the crux of this
debate is to see whether, starting with the same incontesta-
bly individualistic conception of society and using the same
institutional structures, we are able to make a counter-
proposal to the theory of social contract which neo-liberals
want to put into operation, one which would include in its
conditions a principle of distributive justice and which
would hence be compatible with the theoretical and practical tradition of socialism'.[4]

It is no wonder then that Bobbio manifests sympathy for
the proposals of John Rawls in his celebrated book *A Theory
of Justice*, and that he takes Rawls' side against Nozick's
defence of the minimal state in *Anarchy, State and Utopia*.
Bobbio considers that, as long as democracy is alive and that
individuals retain a right to determine the terms of a new
social contact, they will ask not only for the protection of
their fundamental rights and of their property, but also for
a clause concerned with distributive justice.

But will such a new social contract provide the solution, as
Bobbio believes, to the growing ungovernability of modern
industrial societies? Can a social contract that articulates the
demands of social justice with individual civil and political
rights solve the problems facing complex societies today? Is
that the way to get out of what he presents as the paradoxes
of democracy? The communitarian critics of liberalism
think not, and claim that, since liberal individualism is the

cause of the problems, it cannot be the path to their resolution.

In order to assess these claims and to evaluate the adequacy of Bobbio's proposals, we need to examine his diagnosis concerning the situation of democracy and the difficulties which confront it in complex societies.

Bobbio's Conception of Democracy

Bobbio insists, again and again, that we should adopt what he calls a 'minimal definition of democracy' as a form of government 'characterised by a set of rules (primary or basic) which establish *who* is authorised to take collective decisions and *which* procedures are to be applied'.[5] Those 'rules of the game' are designed to facilitate and guarantee the widest participation of the majority of citizens in the decisions which affect the whole of society. The function of some of these rules is to establish what is meant by the general will. They determine who has the right to vote, guarantee that the votes of all citizens have equal weight and specify which type of collective decisions are going to be put into effect. In addition to these three rules, there are others which refer to the conditions that need to be fulfilled in order that the exercise or the freedom to choose be a real one. Of these, there is first the principle of pluralism according to which a democratic system must guarantee the existence of a plurality of organised political groupings which compete with each other; secondly, voters must be able to choose between different alternatives; and finally the minority must be guaranteed the right to become a majority in its turn, through the organisation of periodical electors.

Bobbio, then, chooses to privilege a procedural or juridico-institutional definition of democracy, rather than a substantial, ethical one that stresses the ideal of equality, presented as the objective that a democratic government should strive for. He believes that the most important question for democracy is not 'who rules?' but 'how do they rule?' and that democracy is best understood, in contradistinction to autocracy, as a form of government where power comes from below instead of being imposed from above. It is for this reason that he defends representative democracy as the only adequate model for our modern complex societies and dismisses the calls for direct democracy made by some radical democrats.

To make democracy compatible with liberalism, is thus one of Bobbio's main concerns. He declares, for instance, that 'democracy can be seen as the natural development of liberalism providing that we have in mind not the ideal, egalitarian aspect of democracy, but its character as a political formula in which, as we have seen, it is tantamount to popular sovereignty.'[6] The crucial link, according to him, is located in the articulation between the two sets of rules which are constitutive of the democratic game. As has been indicated above, some of the six procedural rules that Bobbio presents as necessary for a political system to be called democratic refer to the conditions required in order that the exercise of the right to vote be a free one between real alternatives. Bobbio declares that only a liberal state can guarantee the basic rights which such a requisite entails: freedom of opinion, or expression, of speech, of assembly, of association, etc. He comments that

> these are the rights on which the liberal state has been founded since its inception, giving rise to the doctrine of the *Rechtsstaat*, or juridical state, in the full sense of the term, i.e. the state which not only exercises power *sub lege*, but exercises it within the limits derived from the constitutional recognition of the so-called 'inviolable' rights of the individual. Whatever may be the philosophical basis of these rights, they are the necessary precondition for the mainly procedural mechanisms, which characterise a democratic system, to work properly. The constitutional norms which confer these rights are not rules of the game as such; they are preliminary rules which allow the game to take place.[7]

With respect to the present and future conditions of democracy, Bobbio distinguishes between the advances that could be made and the actual difficulties facing democratic societies today. Concerning the latter, he discusses at length what he sometimes calls the 'unfulfilled promises' of democracy, or at other times presents as one of the 'paradoxes of democracy'. These paradoxes relate primarily to the fact that we are asking for more and more democracy in conditions that are increasingly unpropitious, given the growth of large state organisations, the development of technocracy and bureaucracy and the rise of conformism due to the hegemony of mass culture. In Bobbio's terms, the difficulties are the following:

> In a nut-shell, these four enemies of democracy – where I am taking democracy to mean the optimum method for making collective decisions – are the large scale of modern life; the increasing bureaucratisation of the state apparatus; the growing technicality of the decisions it is necessary to make; and the trend of civil society towards becoming a mass society.[8]

The major shortcomings of existing democracies lie in the survival of invisible power, and of oligarchies, the demise of the individual as the protagonist of political life, the renewed vigour of particular interests, the limited space for democratic participation and the failure to create educated citizens. But, apart from one instance of invisible power, where Bobbio sees a trend that contradicts the basic premises of democracy, he considers the other problems as the necessary consequence of adapting abstract principles to reality. Far from seeing direct democracy as a possible solution, he believes that, besides being impossible, it would only make things worse.

What is then the remedy proposed by Bobbio? Can something be done to further the process of democratisation in modern advanced societies? In the end, Bobbio appears moderately optimistic but insists that we should be realistic and abandon all hopes of a 'true democracy', of a perfectly reconciled society, of a perfect consensus. Modern democracy, he insists, must come to terms with pluralism, and this implies that some form of dissent is inevitable. Consensus is necessary, but only as far as the rules of the game are concerned. Those rules, when implemented, are the best guarantees against autocracy and heteronomy that constantly threaten the struggle for autonomy which Bobbio sees as the driving force fo democracy.

Once the illusion of direct democracy has been discarded, says Bobbio, we can begin to envisage how the struggle for more democracy can take place. It can only mean the extension of representative democracy to more and more areas of social life; the central question is not to look for the emergence of a new type of democracy, but for a process 'in which quite traditional forms of democracy, such as representative democracy are infiltrating new spaces, spaces occupied until now by hierarchic or bureaucratic organisations'.[9] In short, we should proceed from the democratisation of the state to the democratisation of society and the task is to struggle against autocratic power in all its forms in order to infiltrate the various spaces still occupied by non-democratic centres of power. To democratise society requires, for Bobbio, tackling all institutions, from family to school, from big business to public administration, which are not run democratically. He declares that

> Nowadays if an indicator of democratic progress is needed it cannot be provided by the number of people who have the right to vote, but the number of contexts outside politics where the right to vote is exercised. A laconic but effective way of putting it is to say that the criterion for judging the state of democratisation achieved in a given country should no longer be to establish 'who' votes, but 'where' they can vote.[10]

Pluralism and Individualism

As we have seen, according to Bobbio liberal socialism can offer a solution to the present shortcomings of democracy by providing a new social contract, which has at its centre a principle of social justice. The aim is to combine social, political and civil rights, putting them on a strong individualistic foundation by appealing to the principle of the individual as the ultimate source of power. The issue of individualism is presented as crucial by Bobbio who

argues that 'Without individualism; there can be no liberalism'.[11] The compatibility of liberalism and democracy lies
for him in the fact that both share a common starting-point
– the individual – and are therefore grounded in an
individualistic conception of society. The modern idea of
the social contact represents, in his view, a Copernican
revolution in the relationship between individual and
society because it indicates the end of an organicist and
holistic conception of society and the birth of individualism.
By placing the particular individual with her interests,
needs and rights at the centre of society, the individualistic
conception made possible not only the liberal state, but also
the modern idea of democracy. Liberal ideas and democratic procedures were therefore interwoven and their com-
bination led to a liberal democracy where 'Liberalism
defends and proclaims individual liberty as against the
state, in both the economic and the social sphere;
democracy reconciles individual and society by making
society the product of a common agreement between
individuals'.[12]

While I agree with Bobbio on the importance of individualism to the birth of the modern conception of society,
it seems to me that we must now question whether such an
individualistic conception has not become an obstacle to the
extension of democratic ideals. Many of the problems that
Bobbio finds in modern democracies could be attributed to
the effects of individualism. For instance, in their critique
of the work of John Rawls, many communitarians have
argued that it is precisely the individualistic conception of
the subject (with rights held previously and independently
of his/her insertion into society) that is at the origin of our
problems. Far from seeing the solution in a new social
contract, they consider that it is the very idea of a social
contract, with all its atomistic implications, that needs to be
abandoned. It is for this reason that they argue for a revival
of the civic republican tradition with its richer conception of
citizenship and its view of politics as the realm where we can
recognize ourselves as participants in a political community
organised around the idea of a shared common good.

I will discuss the adequacy of such a solution later,[13] but at this point I would like to address several specific problems raised by the extension of democracy today, and the failure of the individualistic framework to deal with them. Let me start by indicating my points of convergence with Bobbio. I think that he is right to stress the importance of representative democracy and the need to abandon the illusions of direct democracy and perfect consensus in a completely transparent society. When he declares that democracy in a modern state has no alternative but to be a pluralistic democracy, I could not agree more. But it is precisely for this reason that I see individualism as an obstacle – because it does not allow us to theorise that pluralism in an adequate way. If representative democracy needs to be defended, we must also acknowledge that its theory is really deficient, and that we have to formulate new arguments in its favour. As Carl Schmitt has shown convincingly in his critique of parliamentary democracy, the classical theory of parliamentarism has been made completely obsolete by the development of the interventionist state.[14] Bobbio does in fact seem to agree with such a judgement, since he criticises the classical conception of representation and recognises that no constitutional norm has ever been more violated than the veto on binding mandates. He even does so far as to admit that it could not have been otherwise, and declares,

> Confirmation of the victory – I would dare to say a definitive one – of the representation of interests over impartial political representation is provided by the type of relationship, which is coming to be the norm in most democratic states in Europe, between opposed interest groups (representatives of industrialists and workers respectively) and parliament. This relationship has brought about a new type of social system which is called, rightly or wrongly 'neo-corporatism'.[15]

Nevertheless Bobbio leaves the question at that point and does not provide us with a new rationale for representative democracy, one that would take account of the role played by interest groups. His only argument is that direct democracy would not do better but worse. But this is far from satisfactory, and it does not provide any answer to Schmitt's assertion that

> If in the actual circumstances of parliamentary business, openness and discussion have become an empty and trivial formality, then parliament, as it developed in the nineteenth century, has also lost its previous foundation and its meaning.[16]

To be sure, Bobbio refers to certain developments of democratic theory which have shifted the emphasis from the classical theory of democracy's stress on the ideas of 'participation' and 'sovereignty', to the idea of 'control'. It could indeed be argued that his insistence on a procedural conception of democracy is proof that he situates himself more in the camp of the realist theorists than the classical ones. The problem is that he often combines elements from the two traditions without realising that they can be in conflict. Can one put Schumpeter and Stuart Mill together in the unproblematic way that Bobbio seems to assume? And things get even more complicated when it comes to articulating socialism with this already peculiar mixture. Besides insisting on the necessity of a principle of distributive justice and the need to recognise social rights, Bobbio does not really have much to say on this topic.

To develop solutions to the problems facing liberal democracies today, and to provide an effective articulation between socialist goals and the principles of liberal democracy, it is necessary to overcome the framework of individualism. I am not postulating a return to an organicist and holistic conception of society, which is clearly pre-modern and inadequate for modern democracy. It is rather that I believe that the individualistic conception which is predominant in liberal theory is not the only alternative to such a view. The problem is to theorise the individual, not as a monad, an 'unencumbered' self existing previously to and independently of society, but as constituted by an ensemble of 'subject positions', inscribed in a multiplicity of social relations, member of many communities and participant in a plurality of collective forms of identification.

For that reason the question of both 'representation of interests' and of rights has to be posed in a completely different way. The ideas of social rights, for instance, needs to be envisaged in terms of 'collective rights' that are ascribed to specific communities. It is through her inscription in specific social relations that a social agent is granted rights, not as an individual outside society. Some of these rights can of course be of a universalistic character and correspond to all members of the political community; but some others will only correspond to specific social inscriptions.

What is at stake here is not a rejection of universalism in favour of particularism, but the need for a new type of articulation between the universal and the particular. There is a way in which the abstract universalism of human rights can be used to negate specific identities, and to repress some forms of collective identities corresponding to specific communities. Without returning to a view that denies the universal dimension of the individual and only makes room for pure particularism – which is another form of essentialism – it should be possible to conceive of individuality as constituted by the intersection of a multiplicity of identifications and collective identities that constantly subvert each other.

Citizenship and Pluralism

Individualism is also an obstacle for the elaboration of the new conception of citizenship which is required by the current exigencies of democratic politics. The terms of debate are currently far too restrictive, giving rise to many false dilemmas and political misunderstandings. On one side we have those who defend a 'communitarian' view of politics and a citizenship that privileges a type of community constituted by shared moral values and organised around the idea of 'the common good'. On the other side we have the liberal view which affirms that there is no common good and that each individual should be able to define her own good and realise it in her own way. The communitarians want to revive the civic republican conception of citizenship as the key identity that overrides all others and their approach runs the risk of sacrificing the rights of the individual. For the liberals, on the contrary, our identity as citizens – which is restricted to a legal status and to the possession of a set of rights that we hold against the state – is only one among many others and does not play any privileged role. Politics for them is only the terrain where different groups compete for the promotion of their specific private interests and the very idea of the political community is put into question. In this case it is the citizen which is sacrificed to the individual. Many communitarian critiques have rightly pointed to the disintegration of social bonds and the growing phenomenon of anomie which have accompanied the dominance of the liberal view, resulting in the current dissaffection with political life in Western democracies. But we cannot accept the solution put forward by the communitarians because their attempt to recreate a type of '*gemeinschaft*' community, cemented by a substantive idea of the common good, is clearly pre-modern and incompatible with the pluralism that is constitutive of modern democracy. If one must criticise the shortcomings of liberalism, one should also recognise its crucial contribution to the emergence of a modern conception of democracy. It is therefore important to acknowledge the specificity of modern democracy and the central role played in it by pluralism.

The problem that we are facing can be formulated in this way: how to conceive the political community under modern democratic conditions? Or: how to conceptualise our identities as individuals and as citizens in a way that does not sacrifice one to the other? The question at stake is how to make our belonging to different communities of values, language and culture compatible with our common belonging to a political community whose rules we have to accept. As against conceptions that stress commonality at the expense of plurality and respect for differences, or that deny any form of commonality in the name of plurality and difference, what we need is to envisage a form of commonality that respects diversity and makes room for different forms of individuality.

Citizenship and the Political Community

The central issue concerns the way we conceptualise the political community, and our belonging to it, i.e. citizenship. The political community should be conceived as a discursive surface and not as an empirical referent. Politics is about the constitution of the political community, not something that takes place within it. The political community, as a surface of inscription of a multiplicity of demands, where a 'we' is constituted, requires the correlative idea of the common good, but a common good conceived as a 'vanishing point', something to which we must constantly refer but that can never be reached. In such a view, the common good functions, on the one hand, as a 'social imaginary': that is, as that which is given, by the very impossibility of achieving full representation, the role of a horizon, which is the condition of possibility of any representation within the space that it delimits. On the other hand, the common good specifies what we can call, following Wittgenstein, a 'grammar of conduct' that coincides with the allegiance to the constitutive ethico-political principles of modern democracy: liberty and equality for all. Yet, since those principles are open to many competing interpretations, one has to acknowledge that a fully inclusive political community can never be realised. There will always be a 'constitutive outside', an exterior to the community that is the very condition of its existence. It is crucial to recognise that, to construct a 'we' it is necessary to distinguish it from a 'them', and that all forms of consensus are based on acts of exclusion. Hence the condition of possibility of the political community is at the same time the condition of impossibility of its full realisation.

The previous considerations have important implications for the understanding of our identity as citizens. The perspective that I am proposing envisages citizenship as a form of political identity that is created through identification with the political principles of modern pluralist democracy, i.e. the assertion of liberty and equality for all. By that I mean allegiance to a set of rules and practices that construe a specific language game, the language of modern democratic citizenship. A citizen is not, in this perspective, as in liberalism, someone who is the passive recipient of rights and who enjoys the protection of the law. It is rather a common political identity of persons who might be engaged in many different communities and who have differing conceptions of the good, but who accept submission to certain authoritative rules of conduct. Those rules are not instruments for achieving a common purpose – since the idea of a substantive common good has been discarded – but conditions that individuals must observe in choosing and pursuing purposes of their own. The reflections on civil association developed by Michael Oakeshot, in *On Human Conduct*, are pertinent here, for they can help us formulate the kind of bond that should exist among citizens in a way that reconciles freedom with authority.[17]

For Oakeshott, the participants in a civil association or '*societas*' are linked by the authority of the conditions specifying their common or 'public' concern. These consist in a series of rules, or rule-like prescriptions, that he calls '*respublica*', and that specify not performances but conditions to be accepted in choosing performances. According to such a view, what is required in order to belong to a political community is the acceptance of a specific language of civil intercourse, the '*respublica*'. The identification with those rules creates a common political identity among persons otherwise engaged in many different enterprises and communities. This modern form of political community is held together not by a substantive idea of the common good but by a common bond, a public concern. It is therefore a community without a definite shape and in continuous re-enactment.

If we apply Oakeshott's views to the principles of modern democracy as a new form of political regime, we can say that in a liberal democratic regime, the '*respublica*' is constituted by the political principles of such a regime: equality and liberty for all. By interpreting Oakeshott's notion of the '*respublica*' in this way, we are able to affirm that the conditions to which one must subscribe as a citizen are to be understood as the exigency of treating others as free and equal persons. It is evident, however, that this can be interpreted in many different ways and lead to competing forms of identification. For instance, a radical democratic interpretation will emphasise the numerous social relations where domination exists and must be challenged if the principles of liberty and equality are to apply. Therefore citizenship as a form of political identity cannot be neutral, but will have a variety of forms according to the competing interpretations of the '*respublica*'. The creation of political identities as radical democratic citizens, for instance, depends on a collective form of identification among the democratic demands found in a variety of movements – women, workers, black, gay, ecological – as well as against other forms of subordination. Through this conception of citizenship, a sense of 'we' is created by a recognition that the demands of these various movements can form a chain of democratic equivalence. It must be stressed that such a relation of *equivalence* does not eliminate *difference* – that would be simple identity. It is only insofar as democratic differences are oppposed to forces or discourses which negate all of them that these differences are interchangable. That is, the 'we' of the radical democratic forces is created by the delimitation of a frontier, the designation of the 'them'; it is not an homogeneous 'we', predicated on the identity of its components. Through the principle of equivalence, a type of commonality is created that does not erase plurality and differences, and respects diverse forms of individuality.

Such a view of citizenship is clearly different both from the liberal and the communitarian ones. It is not one identity among others, as it is in liberalism, nor is it the dominant identity that overrides all others, as it is in civic republicanism. It is an articulating principle that affects the different subject positions of the social agent, while allowing for a plurality of specific allegiances and for the respect of individual liberty. A conception of citizenship that allows for the multiplicity of identities that constitute an individual can only be defended by relinquishing the atomistic problematic of individualism, and by recognising that it is only through inscription in a set of social relations that individuality is constructed.

To deepen and enrich the pluralist conquests of liberal democracy, the articulation between political liberalism and individualism must be broken, to make possible a new approach to individuality that restores its social nature without reducing it to a simple component of an organic whole. This is where the socialist tradition of thought might still have something to contribute to the democratic project and herein lies the promise of a liberal socialism.

Notes

[1] Ernesto Laclau and Chantal Mouffe, *Hegemony and Socialist Strategy Towards a Radical Democratic Politics*, Verso, London 1985.

[2] Norberto Bobbio, *The Future of Democracy*, Polity Press, Cambridge 1987, p 25.

[3] This historical background of Bobbio's thought is well analysed in the article by Perry Anderson 'The Affinities of Norberto Bobbio', *New Left Review*, No 170, July-August 1988.

[4] *Ibid*, p 117.

[5] *Ibid*, p 24.

[6] Norberto Bobbio, *Liberalism and Democracy*, Verso, London 1990, p 37.

[7] Bobbio, *The Future of Democracy*, p 25.

[8] Norberto Bobbio, *Which Socialism?*, Polity Press, Cambridge 1987, p 99.

[9] Bobbio, *The Future of Democracy*, p 55.

[10] *Ibid*, p 56.

[11] Bobbio, *Liberalism and Democracy*, p 9.

[12] *Ibid*, p 43.

[13] I have already discussed this issue in two articles: 'American Liberalism and its critics: Rawls, Taylor, Sandel and Walzer', *Praxis International*, 8,2 (July 1988); 'Rawls; Political Philosophy Without Politics', in *Philosophy and Social Criticism*, Vol. 13, No 2, 1987.

[14] Carl Schmitt, *The Crisis of Parliamentary Democracy*, trans. E. Kennedy, Cambridge, Mass./London 1985.

[15] Bobbio, *The Future of Democracy*, p 30.

[16] Schmitt, *op cit*, p 50.

[17] The argument that I am presenting here is developed at greater length in my article 'Democratic Citizenship and the Political Community', in Chantal Mouffe (ed), *Dimensions of Radical Democracy: Pluralism, Citizenship, Community*, Verso, London 1992.

Class Relations, Social Justice and the Politics of Difference

DAVID HARVEY

It is hard to discuss the politics of identity, multiculturalism, 'otherness' and 'difference' in abstraction from
material circumstances and of political project. I shall,
therefore, situate my discussion in the context of a
particular problematic – that of the search for a 'socially
just' social order – within the particular material
circumstances prevailing in the United States today.

Hamlet, North Carolina

In the small town of Hamlet, North Carolina, (population
approximately 6,000), there is a chicken processing plant
run by Imperial Foods. Chicken production is big business
in these times for it can now be mass-produced under
low-cost conditions of industrialised management. For
many of America's poor (hit by declining incomes these
last two decades) it has consequently become a major
source of protein; consumption doubled in the 1980s to
equal that of beef. The conditions prevailing with the
broiler chicken industry, stretched in a vast arc running
from Maryland's Eastern Shore through the Carolinas and
across the deep south into the Texas Panhandle (the zone
known as 'The Broiler Belt' because agricultural incomes
are dominated by the industry), are, however, less than
salubrious (salmonella contamination is an endemic

danger and descriptions of production conditions are liable to stir the ire of those only mildly sensitive to animal rights). Ancillary to broiler-chicken production is a chicken processing industry employing 150,000 workers in 250 or so plants, mostly located in very small towns or rural settings throughout the 'Broiler Belt'.

On Tuesday September 3rd, 1991, the day after the United States celebrated its 'labor day', the Imperial Foods plant in Hamlet caught fire. Many of the exit doors were locked. Twenty five of the two hundred workers employed in the plant died and a further fifty six were seriously injured.

It was a cataclysmic industrial accident, at least by the standards of any advanced industrial country, but it also revealed, as Struck, one of the few journalists to investigate, discovered, some very harsh truths about the 'latest industry of toil to reign in the (American) South.'[1] Those employed in the plant start off at minimum wage ($4.25 an hour) and later progress to $5.60 an hour which translates into take-home pay of less than $200 per week which is below the poverty line for a single-headed household with children. But there is little or no alternative employment in Hamlet, and for this particular town the plant is a vital economic asset precisely because 'for a lot of people, any kind of job is better than no job at all.' Those living in relatively geographically isolated rural towns of this sort are, consequently, easy prey for an industry seeking a cheap, unorganised and easily disciplined labour force. Struck continues his account thus:

> The workers at the Imperial Foods plant describe demeaning conditions with few benefits and no job security. They were routinely cursed by bosses, the employees say. They were allowed only one toilet break from the processing line. A single day off required a doctor's permission. Any infraction was noted as an 'occurrence' and five occurrences would get a worker fired. 'The supervisors treated you like nothing, and all they want you to do is get their chicken out,' said Brenda MacDougald, 36, who had been at the plant two years.

'They treated people like dogs,' said a bitter Alfonso
Anderson. Peggy, his wife of 27 years, died in the fire. She
had worked there for 11 years, despite her complaints.
'Around here, you have to take some stuff and swallow it to
keep a job,' he said, fighting back tears.

North Carolina as a State has long had the habit of
openly touting low wages, a friendly business climate and
'right-to-work' legislation which keeps the unions at bay as
the bait to pull in more and more manufacturing
employment of exactly this sort. The poultry industry as a
whole is estimated to add more than $1.5 billion annually
to North Carolina's economy. In this case, however, the
'friendly business climate', translates into not enforcing
laws on occupational health and safety. North Carolina
'has only 14 health inspectors and 27 safety inspectors
(ranking) lowest in the nation in proportion to the number
of inspectors (114) recommended under federal guidelines.' Federal personnel are supposed, under Congressio-
nal mandate, to make up the difference but none have
visited the plants in North Carolina in recent years. The
Hamlet plant had not, therefore, been inspected in its
eleven years in operation. 'There were no fire
extinguishers, no sprinkler system, no safety exit doors.'
Other plants in the State have rarely been inspected let
alone cited for violations, though fires have been common
and the occupational injury rate in the industry is nearly
three times the national average.

There are a number of compelling reflections which this
incident provokes. First of all, this is a *modern* (i.e. recently
established) industry whose employment conditions could
easily be inserted as a description into Karl Marx's chapter
on 'The Working Day' in *Capital* (published in 1867)
without any one noticing any fundamental difference. It
surely bodes ill (in some sense or other) for the 'free
market triumphalism' to which we are currently exposed
when looking towards the East that such a miserable
equation can so easily be made in the West between
nineteenth century levels of exploitation in Britain and
employment conditions in a recently established industry

in the most powerful advanced industrial capitalist country in the world. The most obvious comparison in the United States is with the Triangle Shirtwaist Company fire of 1911 in which 146 employees died and which led over 100,000 people to march down Broadway in protest and which became the cause celebre for the labour movement to fight for better workplace protection. Yet, as Davidson notes, 'despite a dizzying matrix of laws, regulations and codes enacted to protect workers, most of the Imperial workers died as the women in New York had: pounding desperately on locked or blocked fire doors.'[2]

The second reflection is that we should pay close attention to the industrial structures developing in rural and small-town settings in the United States, for it is here where the decline of agricultural employment (to say nothing of the rash of farming bankruptcies) over the past decades or so has left behind a relatively isolated industrial reserve army (again, of the sort which Marx described so well in *Capital* – see chapter 25 section 5, for example) which is far more vulnerable to exploitation than its urban counterpart. American industry has long used spatial dispersal and the geographical isolation of employees as one of its prime mechanisms of labour control (in industries like chicken processing and meat packing the equation is obvious but this principle is also deployed in electronics and other supposedly ultra-modern industries). But recent transformations in industrial organisation, flexible locational choices and deregulation have here been turned into a totally unsubtle form of coercive exploitation which is pre- rather than post-Fordist in its organisational form.

This leads to a third reflection concerning the dismantling, through deindustrialisation and industrial reorganisation over the last two decades, of many of the forces and institutions of 'traditional' (i.e. blue collar and unionised) working class forms of power. The dispersal and creation of many new jobs in rural settings has facilitated capitalist control over labour by searching out non-unionised and pliable workforces. The manufacturing sectors of central cities, which have always been more vulnerable to expressions of organised discontent or political regulation, have been reduced to zones of either high unemployment (cities like Chicago, New York, Los Angeles and Baltimore have seen their traditional blue collar manufacturing employment cut in half in the last twenty years) or of unorganised sweatshop-style industries. The non-financial zones of inner cities, which have quite rightly been the focus of so much attention in the past, have increasingly become, therefore, centres of *un*employment and *oppression* (of the sort which led to the recent explosion in Los Angeles) rather than creatures of labour *exploitation* and working class political organisation of the classic sort.

But the immediate matter I wish to concentrate attention upon here, is the general lack of political response to this cataclysmic event. For while the Triangle Shirtwaist Company fire provoked a massive protest demonstration at the beginning of the twentieth century in New York City, the fire in Hamlet, North Carolina at the end of the twentieth century received hardly any media or political attention, even though some labour groups and political organisations (such as Jackson's Rainbow Coalition) did try to focus attention upon it as a matter of ethical and moral urgency. The interesting contrast in September of 1991, was with the Clarence Thomas Supreme Court nomination hearings which became a major focus for a great deal of political agitation and action as well as of media debate. These hearings, it should be noted, focussed on serious questions over race and gender relations in a *professional* rather than *working class* context. It is also useful to contrast events in Hamlet, North Carolina, with those in Los Angeles, in which *oppression* as expressed in the beating of Rodney King on a highway and the failure to convict the police officers involved, sparked a virtual urban uprising of the underprivileged, while the deaths of twenty-six people through *exploitation* in a rural factory setting provoked almost no reaction at all.

Those contrasts become even more significant when it is realised that of the twenty five people who died in the

Hamlet fire, eighteen were women and twelve were African-American. This is not, apparently, an uncommon profile of employment structure throughout the 'Broiler Belt', though Hispanics would typically substitute for African-Americans in the Texas Panhandle sector in particular. The commonality that cuts across race and gender lines in this instance is quite obviously that of class and it is hard not to see the immediate implication that a simple, traditional form of class politics could have protected the interests of women and minorities as well as those of white males. And this in turn raises important questions of exactly what kind of politics, what definition of social justice and of ethical and moral responsibility, is adequate to the protection of such exploited populations irrespective of their race and gender. The thesis I shall explore here is that it was raw class politics of an exploitative sort which created a situation in which an accident (a fire) could have the effects it did. For what happened in Hamlet, North Carolina, Struck surmised, was 'an accident waiting to happen.'

Consider, first, the general history of workplace safety and of regulatory practices and enforcements in the United States. Labour struggles around events such as the Triangle Shirtwaist Company fire put occupational safety and health very much upon the political agenda during the 1920s and it was a fundamental feature of Roosevelt's New Deal coalition, which included the labour unions, to try to satisfy some minimum requirements on this score without alienating business interests. The National Labor Relations Board acquired powers to regulate class conflict in the workplace (including conflicts over safety) as well as to specify the legal conditions under which unions (which would often take on health and safety issues directly) could be set up. But it was not until 1970 that a Democratically controlled Congress consolidated the bits and pieces of legislation that had accumulated from New Deal days onwards into the organisation of the Occupational Safety and Health Administration (OSHA) with real powers to regulate business practices in the work place. This legislation was, it should be noted, part of a package of reforms which set up the Environmental Protection Agency, The Consumer Product Safety Commission, the National Traffic Safety Commission and the Mine and Safety Health Administration, all of which signalled a much greater preparedness of a Democratically-controlled Congress in the early 1970s to enact legislation (in spite of a Republican President) that would extend state powers to intervene in the economy.

I think it important to recognise the conditions which led the Democratic Party, a political party which from the New Deal onwards sought to absorb but never to represent, let alone become an active instrument of, working class interests, to enact legislation of such an interventionist character. The legislation was not, in fact, an outcome of the class and sectional alliance politics which had created the New Deal, but came at the tail-end of a decade in which politics had shifted from universal programmes (like Social Security) to specially targeted programmes to help regenerate the inner cities (e.g. Model Cities and Federally-funded housing programmes), take care of the elderly or the particularly impoverished (e.g. Medicare and Medicaid), and target particular disadvantaged groups in the population (Headstart and Affirmative action). This shift from universalism to targeting of particular groups inevitably created tensions between groups and helped fragment rather than consolidate any broader sense of a progressive class alliance. Each piece of legislation which emerged in the early 1970s appealed to a different group (unions, environmentalists, consumer advocacy groups, and the like). Nevertheless, the net effect was to create a fairly universal threat of intervention in the economy from many special interest groups and in certain instances – OSHA in particular – in the realm of production.

The latter is, of course, very dangerous territory upon which to venture. For while it is accepted, even by the most recalcitrant capitalist interests, that the State always has a fundamental role in ensuring the proper functioning of the market and respect for private property rights, interventions in that 'hidden abode' of production in which the secret of profit making resides, is always deeply resisted, as Marx long ago pointed out, by capitalist class interests.[3] This treading on the hallowed ground of the prerogatives of business provoked an immediate political repsonse. Edsall early on spotted its direction:

> During the 1970s, business refined its ability to act as a class, submerging competitive instincts in favor of joint, cooperative action in the legislative arena. Rather than individual companies seeking only special favors ... the dominant theme in the political strategy of business became a shared interest in the defeat of bills such as consumer protection and labor law reform, and in the enactment of favorable tax, regulatory and antitrust legislation.[4]

In acting as a class, business increasingly used its financial power and influence (particularly through political action committees) during the 1970s and 1980s, to effectively capture the Republican Party as its class instrument and forge a coalition against all forms of government intervention (save those advantageous to itself) as well as against the welfare state (as represented by government spending and taxation). This culminated in the Reagan administration's policy initiatives which centered on an:

> across-the-board drive to reduce the scope and content of the federal regulation of industry, the environment, the workplace, health care, and the relationship between buyer and seller. The Reagan administration's drive toward deregulation was accomplished through sharp budget cuts reducing enforcement capabilities; through the appointment of anti-regulatory, industry-oriented agency personnel; and, finally, through the empowering of the Office of Management and Budget with unprecedented authority to delay major regulations, to force major revisions in regulatory proposals, and through prolonged cost-benefit analyses, to effectively kill a wide range of regulatory initiatives.[5]

This willingness of the Republican party to become the representative of 'its dominant class constituency' during this period contrasted with the 'ideologically ambivalent' attitude of the Democrats which grew out of 'the fact that its ties to various groups in society are diffuse, and none of these groups – women, blacks, labor, the elderly, Hispanics, urban political organizations – stands clearly larger than the others.'[6] The dependency of Democrats, furthermore, upon 'big money' contributions rendered many of them also highly vulnerable to direct influence from business interests.

The outcome was predictable enough. When a relatively coherent class force encounters a fragmented opposition which cannot even conceive of its interests in class terms, then the result is hardly in doubt. Institutions like the National Labor Relations Board and OSHA were crippled or turned around to fit business rather than labour agendas. Moody notes, for example, that by 1983 it took on average 627 days for the NLRB to issue a decision on an unfair labour practice, which is an impossible time to wait if the unfair labour practice involves dismissal and the person dismissed has nothing to live on in the meantime.[7] It was this political and administrative climate of total disregard for laws governing labour rights and occupational health and safety which set the stage for that 'accident waiting to happen' at Hamlet, North Carolina.

The failure to register political anger of that sort which followed the Triangle Shirtwaist Company fire in 1911 in New York City also deserves some comment. A similar event in a relatively remote rural setting posed immediate logistical problems for massive on-the-spot political responses (such as the protest demonstration on Broadway), illustrating the effectiveness of capitalist strategies of geographical dispersal away from politicised central city locations as a means of labour control. The only other path to a generalised political response lay in widespread media attention and public debate – surely, given modern communications technology, a very real possibility. But here the other element to the situation prevailing in 1991 came into play. Not only were the working class institutions which might have taken up the cause greatly weakened, both in their ability to react as well as in their access to the media, but the very idea of any kind of working-class politics was likewise on the defensive (if not downright discredited in certain 'radical' circles), even though capitalist class interests and the captive Republican Party had been waging a no-holds-barred and across-the-board class war against the least privileged sectors of the population for the previous two decades.

This weakening of working-class politics in the United States from the mid 1970s on can be tracked back to many causes which cannot be examined in detail here. But one contributory feature has been the increasing fragmentation of 'progressive' politics around special issues and the rise of the so-called new social movements focussing on gender, race, ethnicity, ecology, multiculturalism, community, and the like. These movements often became a working and practical alternative to class politics of the traditional sort and in some instances have exhibited downright hostility to such politics.

I think it instructive here to note that as far as I know, none of the institutions associated with such new social movements saw fit to engage politically with what happened in Hamlet, North Carolina. Women's organisations, for example, were heavily preoccupied with the question of sexual harassment and mobilising against the Clarence Thomas appointment, even though it was mainly women who died in the North Carolina fire and women who continue to bear an enormous burden of exploitation in the 'Broiler Belt'. And apart from the Rainbow coalition and Jesse Jackson, African-American (and Hispanic) organisations also remained strangely silent on the matter, while some ecologists (particularly the animal rights wing) exhibited more sympathy for the chickens than for the workers. The general tone in the media, therefore, was to sensationalise the horror of the 'accident', but not to probe at all into its origins and certainly not to indite capitalist class interests, the Republican Party, the failures of the State of North Carolina or OSHA as accessory to a murderously negligent event.

The Postmodern Death of Justice

According to most common sense meanings of the word, many of us would accept that the conditions under which men, women and minorities work in the Hamlet plant are socially unjust. Yet to make such a statement presupposes that there are some universally agreed upon norms as to what we do or ought to mean by the concept of social justice and that no barrier exists, other than the normal ambiguities and fuzziness, to applying the full force of such a powerful principle to the circumstances of North Carolina. But 'universality' is a word which conjurs up doubt and suspicion, downright hostility even, in these 'postmodern' times; the belief that universal truths are both discoverable and applicable as guidelines for political-economic action is nowadays often held to be the chief sin of 'the Enlightenment project' and of the 'totalising' and 'homogenising' modernism it supposedly generated.

The effect of the postmodern critique of universalism has been to render any application of the concept of social justice problematic. And there is an obvious sense in which this questioning of the concept is not only proper but imperative – too many colonial peoples have suffered at the hands of Western imperialism's particular justice, too many African-Americans have suffered at the hands of the white man's justice, too many women from the justice imposed by a patriarchal order and too many workers from the justice imposed by capitalists, to make the concept anything other than problematic. But does this imply that the concept is useless or that to dub events at Hamlet, North Carolina as 'unjust' has no more force than some localised and contingent complaint?

The difficulty of working with the concept is compounded further by the variety of idealist and philosophical interpretations put upon the term throughout the long history of western thought on the matter. There are multiple competing theories of social justice and each has its flaws and strengths. Egalitarian views, for example, immediately run into the problem that 'there is nothing more unequal than the equal treatment of unequals, (the modification of doctrines of equality of opportunity in the United States by requirements for affirmative action, for example, have recognised the historical force of that problem). Positive law theories (whatever the law says is just), utilitarian views (the greatest good of the greatest number), social contract and natural right views, together with the various intuitionist, relative deprivation, and other interpretations of justice, all compete for our attention, leaving us with the conundrum: *which* theory of social justice is the most socially just?

Social justice, for all of the universalism to which proponents of a particular version of it might aspire, has long turned out to be a rather heterogeneous set of concepts. To argue for a particular definition of social justice has always implied, therefore, appeal to some higher order criteria to define which theory of social justice is more appropriate or more just than another. An infinite regress of argument immediately looms as does, in the other direction, the relative ease of deconstruction of any notion of social justice as meaning anything whatsoever, except whatever individuals or groups, given their multiple identities and functions, at some particular moment find it pragmatically, instrumentally, emotionally, politically, or ideologically useful to mean.

At this point there seem two ways to go with the argument. The first is to look at how the multiple concepts of justice are embedded in language and this leads to theories of meaning of the sort which Wittgenstein advanced and which have had such an important impact upon postmodern ways of thought:

> How many kinds of sentence are there? ... There are *countless* kinds: countless different kinds of use to what we call 'symbols', 'words', 'sentences'. And this multiplicity is not something fixed, given once for all: but new types of language, new language games, as we may say, come into existence and others become obsolete and get forgotten ... Here the term 'language-*game*' is meant to bring into prominence the fact that the *speaking* of language is

> part of an activity, or a form of life ... How did we *learn* the meaning of this word ('good' for instance)? From what sort of examples? in what language games? Then it will be easier for us to see that the word must have a family of meanings.[8]

From this perspective, social justice has no universal agreed upon meaning, but a 'family' of meanings which can be understood only through the way each is embedded in a particular language game. But we should note two things about Wittgenstein's formulation. First, the appeal to a 'family' of meanings suggests some kind of interrelatedness and we should presumably pay attention to what those relations might be. Secondly, each language game attaches to the particular social, communicative, experiential and perceptual world of the speaker. The upshot is to bring us to a point of cultural, linguistic or discourse relativism of some sort, albeit based upon the material circumstances of the subject. We should also, then, pay careful attention to those material circumstances.

The second path is to admit the relativism of discourses about justice, but to insist that discourses are expressions of social power and that the 'family' of meanings derives its interrelatedness precisely through the nature of power relations pertaining within and between different social formations. The simplest version of this idea is to interpret social justice as embedded in the hegemonic discourses of any ruling class or ruling faction. This is an idea which goes back to Plato who, in the *Republic* has Thrasymachus argue that:

> Each ruling class makes laws that are in its own interest, a democracy democratic laws, a tyranny tyrannical ones and so on; and in making these laws they define as 'right' for their subjects what is in the interest of themselves, the rulers, and if anyone breaks their laws he is punished as a 'wrong-doer'. That is what I mean when I say that 'right' is the same in all states, namely the interest of the established ruling class ...[9]

Marx and Engels make a similar argument. The latter, for example, writes:

> The stick used to measure what is right and what is not is the most abstract expression of right itself, namely *justice* ... The development of right for the jurists ... is nothing more than a striving to bring human conditions, so far as they are expressed in legal terms, ever closer to the ideal of justice, *eternal* justice. And always this justice is but the ideologized, glorified expression of the existing economic relations, now from their conservative and now from their revolutionary angle. The justice of the Greeks and Romans held slavery to be just; the justice of the bourgeois of 1789 demanded the abolition of feudalism on the ground it was unjust. The conception of eternal justice, therefore, varies not only with time and place, but also with the persons concerned ... While in everyday life ... expressions like right, wrong, justice, and sense of right are accepted without misunderstanding even with reference to social matters, they create ... the same hopeless confusion in any scientific investigation of economic relations as would be created, for instance, in modern chemistry if the terminology of the phlogiston theory were to be retained.[10]

From this it follows that the 'situatedness' or 'standpoint' of whoever makes the argument is relevant if not determinant to understanding the particular meaning put upon the concept. Sentiments of this sort have been taken much further in the postmodern literature. 'Situatedness', 'otherness' and 'positionality' (usually understood in the first instance in terms of class, gender, race, ethnicity, sexual preference, and community, though in some formulations even these categories are viewed with suspicion) here become crucial elements in defining how particular differentiated discourses (be they about social justice or anything else) arise and how such discourses are put to use as part of the play of power. There can be no universal conception of justice to which we can appeal as a normative concept to evaluate some event, such as the Imperial Foods plant fire. There are only particular, competing, fragmented and heterogeneous conceptions of and discourses about justice which arise out of the particular situations of those involved. The task of deconstruction and of postmodern criticism is to reveal how *all* discourses about social justice hide power relations. The effect of this postmodern extension of Engels' line of reasoning is well described by White. According to White, postmodernists argue:

> that we are far too ready to attach the word 'just' to cognitive, ethical, and political arrangements that are better understood as phenomena of power that oppress, neglect, marginalize, and discipline others. In unmasking such claims about justice, postmodern thinkers imply that their work serves some more valid but unspecified notion of justice. One sees this in Derrida's declaration that 'Deconstruction is justice', but also in his cautioning that one can neither speak directly about nor experience justice. In answering the sense of responsibility to otherness, one serves justice but one does so with a sense of the infinite, open-ended character of the task.[11]

The effect, however, is to produce 'a rather simple bipolar world: deconstructionists and other postmoderns who struggle for justice, and traditional ethical and political theoriests who are the ideologues of unjust orders.' And this in turn produces a serious dilemma for all forms of postmodern argumentation:

> On the one hand, its epistemological project is to deflate all totalistic, universalistic efforts to theorize about justice and the good life; and yet on the other hand, its practical project is to generate effective resistance to the present dangers of totalizing, universalizing rationalization pro-cesses in society. In short, the source of much injustice in contemporary society is seen as general and systematic; the response, however, bars itself from normatively confront-ing the problem on a comparable level by employing a theory of justice offering universally valid, substantive principles. Postmodern reflection thus seems to deny itself just the sort of normative armament capable of conducting a successful fight.[12]

We can see precisely this difficulty emerging in the circumstances that led up to events in Hamlet, North Carolina. When business organised itself as a class to attack government regulation and intervention, and the welfare state (with its dominant notions of social rationality and just redistributions) it did so in the name of the unjust and unfair regulation of private property rights and the unfair taxation of the proper fruits of entrepreneurial endeavour in freely functioning markets. Just deserts, it has long been argued by the ideologues of free-market capitalism (from Adam Smith onwards), are best arrived at through competitively organised, price-fixing markets in which entrepreneurs are entitled to hang onto the profit engendered by their endeavours. There is then no need for explicit theoretical, political, or social argument over what is or is not socially just because social justice is whatever is delivered by the market. Each 'factor' of production (land, labour and capital), for example, will receive its marginal rate of return, its just reward, according to its contribution to production. The role of government should be confined to making sure that markets function freely (e.g. by curbing monopoly powers) and that they are 'properly organised' (which may extend to compensating for clear cases of market failure in, for example, the case of un-priced externalities such as environmental pollution and health hazards). It does not, of course, take that much sophistication to deconstruct this conception of justice as a manifestation of a particular kind of political-economic power. Yet there is widespread, perhaps even hegemonic acceptance of such a standpoint as the numerous 'tax revolts' in the United States over the last decades have shown. From this standpoint, the incident in North Carolina can be interpreted as an unfortunate accident, perhaps compounded by managerial error, in a basically just system which (a) provides employment where there otherwise would be none at wages determined by the demand and supply conditions prevailing in the local labour market, and (b) fills the shops (contrast the ex-Soviet Union) with a vast supply of cheap protein which poor people can for the most part afford to buy. Insofar as this doctrine of just deserts in the market place is ideologically hegemonic, protest in the North Carolina case would be minimised and confined simply to an enquiry into who it was that locked the doors. The lack of response to the Hamlet case can therefore be interpreted as an indication of precisely how dominant such a notice of justice is in the United States today.

The obvious discourse with which to confront such arguments resides in doctrines of workers' rights and the whole rhetoric of class struggle against exploitation, profit-making and worker disempowerment. Neither Marx nor Engels would here eschew *all* talk of rights and justice. While they clearly recognise that these concepts take on different meanings across space and time and according to persons, the exigencies of class relations inevitably produce, as Marx argues in the case of the fight between capital and labour over the proper length of the working day, 'an antinomy, right against right, both equally bearing the seal of the law of exchanges.'[13] Between such *equal* rights (that of the capitalist and that of the worker) 'force decides'. What is at stake here, is not the arbitration between competing claims according to some universal principle of justice, but class struggle over the particular conception of justice and rights which shall be applied to a given situation. In the North Carolina case, had the rights of workers to be treated with respect under conditions of reasonable economic security and safety and with adequate remuneration been properly respected, then the incident almost certainly would not have happened. And if all workers (together with the unemployed) were accorded the same rights and if the exorbitant rates of profit in broiler chicken processing (as well as in other industries) had been curbed, then the importance of the relatively low-price of this source of protein for the poor would have been significantly diminished.

The problem, however, is that such working class rhetoric on rights and justice is as open to criticism and deconstruction as its capitalistic equivalent. Concentration on class alone is seen to hide, marginalise, disempower, repress and perhaps even oppress all kinds of 'others' precisely because it cannot and does not acknowledge explicitly the existence of heterogeneities and differences based on, for example, race, gender, sexuality, age, ability, culture, locality, ethnicity, religion, community, consumer preferences, group affiliation, and the like. Open-ended responsibility to all of these multiple othernesses makes it difficult if not impossible to respond to events in North Carolina with a single institutionalised discourse which might be maximally effective in confronting the rough justice of capitalism's political economy at work in the Broiler Belt.

We have encounter a situation with respect to discourses about social justice which closely matches the political paralysis exhibited in the failure to respond to the North Carolina fire. Politics and discourses both seem to have become so mutually fragmented that response is inhibited. The upshot appears to be a double injustice: not only do men and women, whites and African-Americans die in a preventable event, but we are simultaneously deprived of any normative principles of justice whatsoever by which to condemn or indite the responsible parties.

The Resurrection of Social Justice

There are abundant signs of discontent with the impasse into which postmodernism's and post-structuralism's approach to the question of social justice has fallen. And a number of different strategies have emerged to try to resurrect the mobilising power of arguments about justice in ways which either permit appeal to carefully circumscribed but nevertheless general principles or which, more ambitiously, try to build a bridge between the supposed universalisms of modernism and the frag- mented particularities left behind by post-structuralist deconstructions. I note, for example, Walzer's attempt to pluralise the concept of justice as equality so as to respect the cultural creations of others,[14] and Peffer's attempt to construct principles of social justice which are consistent with Marxist social theory as an antidote to that wing of Marxism which regards all talk of justice and of rights as a pernicious bourgeois trap.[15] From multiple directions, then, there emerges a strong concern to re-instate concern for social justice and to re-elaborate upon what it takes to create the values and institutions of a reasonably just society.

I think it important at the outset to concede the seriousness of the radical intent of post-structuralism to 'do justice' in a world of infinite heterogeneity and open-endedness. Their reasons for refusing to apply universal principles rigidly across heterogeneous situations are not without considerable weight. This alerts us to the unfortunate ways in which many social movements in the twentieth century have foundered on the belief that because their cause is just they cannot possibly themselves behave unjustly. The warning goes even deeper: the application of *any* universal principle of social justice across heterogeneous situations is certain to entail some injustice to someone, somewhere. But, on the other hand, at the end of a road of infinite heterogeneity and open-endedness about what justice might mean, there lies at best a void or at worst a rather ugly world in which the needs of rapists (a particular form of 'otherness' after all) are 'negotiated' or even regarded as 'just' on equivalent terms with those of their victims. Affirming the importance of infinite heterogeneity and open-endedness directly connects to the charge against post-structuralism that it is an 'anything goes' way of thinking within which no particular moral or ethical principles can carry any particular weight over any other. 'At some point,' says White, 'one must have a way of arguing that not all manifestations of otherness should be fostered; some ought to be constrained.'[16] And this presumes some general principles of right or justice.

There is, White goes on to assert, often a tacit admission of such a problem in some of post-structuralism's founding texts. Foucault, having argued strenuously that we can never disentangle 'mechanisms of discipline' from principles of right, ends up raising the possibility of 'a new form of right, one which must be anti-disciplinarian, but at the same time liberated from the principle of sovereignty.'[17] Lyotard likewise argues explicitly for the creation of a 'pristine' but 'non-consensual' notion of justice in *The Postmodern Condition*.[18] And Derrida is deeply concerned about ethics. But in no case are we told much about what, for example, a 'new form of right' might mean.

Initiatives have consequently emerged to try to resurrect some general principles of social justice while attending to post-structuralist criticisms of universalising theory which marginalises 'others'. There are two particular lines of argument which appear to be potentially fruitful.

1. *Breaking out of the local*

The first line derives from the observation that most post-structuralist critical interventions tend to confine their radicalising politics to social interactions occurring 'below the threshold where the systemic imperatives of power and money become so dominant'. The politics of resistance which they indicate are typically attached to small-scale communities of resistance, marginalised groups, abnormal discourses, or simply to that zone of personal life sometimes termed 'the life world' which can be identified as distinct from and potentially resistant to penetration by the rationalising, commodified, technocratic and hence alienating organisation of contemporary capitalism. It is hard to read this literature without concluding that the objective of reform or revolutionary transformation of contemporary capitalism as a whole has been given up on, even as a topic for discussion, let alone as a focus for political organisation. This 'opting out' from consideration of a whole range of questions is perhaps best signalled by the marked silence of most postmodern and post-structuralist thinkers when it comes to critical discussion of any kind of political economy, let alone that of the Marxian variety. The best that can be hoped for, as someone like Foucault seems to suggest, is that innumerable localised struggles might have some sort of collective effect on how capitalism works in general.

Dissatisfaction with such a politics has led some socialist feminists in particular to seek ways to broaden the terrain of struggle beyond the world of face-to-face communalism and into battles over such matters as welfare state policy, public affairs, political organisation via, in Fraser's case, 'an ethic of solidarity' and, in Young's case, through explicit statement of norms of social justice.[20]

Young, for example, complains that the attempt to counter 'the alienation and individualism we find hegemonic in capitalist patriarchal society,' has led feminist groups 'impelled by a desire for closeness and mutual identification,' to construct an ideal of community 'which generates borders, dichotomies, and exclusions' at the same time as it homogenises and represses difference within the group.[21] She explicitly turns the tools of deconstruction against such ideals of community in order to show their oppressive qualities:

> Racism, ethnic chauvinism, and class devaluation, I suggest, grow partly from a desire for community, that is from the desire to understand others as they understand themselves and from the desire to be understood as I understand myself. Practically speaking, such mutual understanding can be approximated only within a homogeneous group that defines itself by common attributes. Such common identification, however, entails reference also to those excluded. In the dynamics of racism and ethnic chauvinism in the United States today, the positive identification of some groups is often achieved by first defining other groups as the other, the devalued semihuman.[22]

Young, however, 'parts ways' with Derrida because she thinks it 'both possible and necessary to pose alternative conceptualizations.' The first step to her argument is to insist that individuals be understood as 'heterogeneous and decentered' (see below). No social group can be truly unitary in the sense of having members who hold to a singular identity. Young strives on this basis to construct some norms of behaviour in the public realm. Our conception of social justice 'requires not the melting away of differences, but institutions that promote reproduction of and respect for group differences without oppression.'[23] We must reject 'the concept of universality as embodied in republican versions of Enlightenment reason' precisely because it sought to 'suppress the popular and linguistic heterogeneity of the urban public.'[24] 'In open and accessible public spaces and forums, one should expect to encounter and hear from those who are different, whose social perspectives, experience and affiliations are different.'

The ideal to which she appeals is 'openness to unassimilated otherness.' This entails the celebration of the distinctive cultures and characteristics of different groups and of the diverse group identities which are themselves perpetually being constructed and deconstructed out of the flows and shifts of social life. But we here encounter a major problem. In modern mass urban society, the multiple mediated relations which constitute that society across time and space are just as important and as 'authentic' as unmediated face-to-face relations. It is just as important for a politically responsible person to know about and respond politically to all those people who daily put breakfast upon our table, even though market exchange hides from us the conditions of life of the producers.[25] When we eat chicken, we relate to workers we never see of the sort that died in Hamlet, North Carolina. Relationships between individuals get mediated through market functions and state powers, and we have to define conceptions of justice capable of operating across and through these multiple mediations. But this is the realm of politics which postmodernism typically avoids.

Young here proposes 'a family of concepts and conditions' relevant to a contemporary conception of social justice. She identifies 'five faces of oppression' which are *exploitation* (the transfer of the fruits of the labour from one group to another, as, for example, in the cases of workers giving up surplus value to capitalists or women in the domestic sphere transferring the fruits of their labour to men), *marginalization* (the expulsion of people from useful particpation in social life so that they are 'potentially subjected to severe material deprivation and even extermination'), *powerlessness* (the lack of that 'authority, status, and sense of self' which would permit a person to be listened to with respect), *cultural imperialism* (stereotyping in behaviours as well as in various forms of cultural expression such that 'the oppressed group's own experience and interpretation of social life finds little expression that touches the dominant culture, while that same culture imposes on the oppressed group its experience and interpretation of social life'); and *violence* (the fear and actuality of random, unprovoked attacks, which have 'no motive except to damage, humiliate, or destroy the person'). I would want to add a further dimension concerning freedom from the oppressive *ecological consequences* of other's actions.

This multi-dimensional conception of social justice is extremely useful. It alerts us to the existence of a 'long social and political frontier' of political action to roll back multiple oppressions. It also emphasises the heterogeneity of experience of injustice – someone unjustly treated in the workplace can act oppressively in the domestic sphere and the victim of that may, in turn, resort to cultural imperialism against others. Yet there are many situations, such as those in Hamlet, North Carolina, where multiple forms of oppression coalesce. Young's conception of a just society combines, therefore, the requirement of freedom from these different forms of oppression (occurring in mediated as well as in face-to-face situations) with 'openness to unassimilated otherness'. But:

> The danger in affirming difference is that the implementa-tion of group-conscious policies will reinstate stigma and exclusion. In the past, group-conscious policies were used to separate those defined as different and exclude them from access to the rights and privileges enjoyed by dominant groups...Group-conscious policies cannot be used to justify exclusion of or discrimination against members of a group in the exercise of general political and civil rights. A democratic cultural pluralism thus requires a dual system of rights: a more general system of rights which are the same for all, and a more specific system of group-conscious policies and rights.[26]

The double meaning of universality then becomes plain: 'universality in the sense of the participation and inclusion of everyone in moral and social life does not imply universality in the sense of adoption of a general point of view that leaves behind particular affiliations, feelings, commitments, and desires.'[27] Universality is no longer rejected out of hand, but reinserted in a dialectical relation to particularity, positionality and group difference. But what constitutes this universality?

2. *Situating 'situated knowledges'*

The second line of development derives from reflection on what it means to say that all knowledges (including conceptions of social justice and of social needs) are 'situated' in a heterogeneous world of difference. 'Situatedness' can be construed, however, in different ways. What I shall term the 'vulgar' conception of it dwells almost entirely on the relevance of individual biographies: I see, interpret, represent and understand the world the way I do because of the particularities of my life history. The separateness of language games and discourses is emphasised, and difference is treated as biographically and sometimes even institutionally, socially, historically, and geographically determined. It proceeds as if none of us can throw off even some of the shackles of personal history or internalise what the condition of being 'the other' is all about and leads to an exclusionary politics of the sort that Young rejects. And it is frequently used as a rhetorical device either to enhance the supposed authenticity and moral authority of one's own accounts of the world or to deny the veracity of other accounts ('since she is black and female of rural origins she cannot possibly have anything authentic to say about conditions of life of the white bourgeoisie in New York City' or, more commonly, 'because he is a white, male, western, heterosexual he is bound to be tied to a certain vision of how the world works'). Individual biographies do, of course, matter and all sorts of problems arise when someone privileged (like myself) purports to speak for or even about others. This is a difficult issue for contemporary social science and philosophy to confront, as Spivak shows.[28] But a relativist, essentialist and non-dialectical view of situatedness generates immense political difficulties. I would not be permitted to speak about the experiential horror of the North Carolina fire, for example, because I am not working class, nor a woman, nor an African-American (nor, for that matter, was I killed in it). Economically secure professional white feminists could not, likewise, speak for any woman whose situation is different. No one in fact could assume the right or obligation to speak for 'others' let alone against the oppression of anyone whose identity is construed as 'other'.

There is, however, a far profounder and more dialectical sense of 'situatedness' to which we can appeal. In Hegel's parable of the master and the slave, for example, situatedness is not seen as *separate and unrelated* difference, but as a *dialectical power relation* between the oppressed and the oppressor. Marx appropriated and radically transformed the Hegelian dialectic in his examination of the relation between capital and labour; his long and critical engagement with bourgeois philosophy and political economy then became the means to define an alternative subaltern and subversive science situated from the perspective of the proletariat. Feminist writers such as Haraway and Harstock examine gender difference and ground their feminist theory in a similar way.[29]

Such a dialectical conception pervades Derrida's view of the individual subject as someone who has no solid identity, but who is a bundle of heterogeneous and not necessarily coherent impulses and desires. Multiple forms of interaction with the world construct individuals as 'a play of difference that cannot completely be comprehended'.[30] 'Otherness' is thereby necessarily internalised within the self. 'Situatedness' is then taken out of its wooden attachment to identifiable individuals and their biographies and is itself situated as a play of difference. When I eat Kentucky-fried chicken, I am situated at one point in a chain of commodity production that leads right back to Hamlet, North Carolina. When I interact with my daughter, I am inevitably caught in a game of the construction of gender identities. When I refrain from using bait to destroy the slugs that have eaten every flower I have nurtured, then I situate myself in an ecological chain of existence. Individuals are heterogeneously constructed subjects internalising 'otherness' by virtue of their relations to the world. Spivak's answer to the whole dilemma of political representation of the other then rests on invoking Derrida's call to render 'delirious that interior voice that is the voice of the other in us.'[31]

Unfortunately, this does not exhaust the problem for, as Ricoeur notes, our own sense of self-hood and of identity in part gets constructed through the narrative devices which we use to describe our temporal relation to the world, and so assumes relatively durable configurations.[32] While identity does not rest upon sameness or essence, it does acquire durability and permanence according to the stories we tell ourselves and others about our history. Although identity internalises otherness, it nevertheless delimits and renders relatively durable both the field of 'othernesses' brought into play and the relation of those others to a particular sense of self-hood. Whites may construct their identity through historical development of a particular relation to blacks, for example; indeed, both groups may use the other to construct themselves. This intertwining of black and white identities in American history was, as Gates has recently show, fundamental to James Baldwin's conception of race relations.[33] But it is precisely by such means that much of the racial problematic of contemporary culture resides.

Nevertheless, we can, from this dialectical perspective, better appreciate Hartsock's claim that 'attention to the epistemologies of situated knowledges,' can 'expose and clarify the theoretical bases for political alliance and solidarity' at the same time as it provides 'important alternatives to the dead-end oppositions set up by postmodernism's rejection of the Enlightenment.[34] We must pay close attention to the 'similarities that can provide the basis for differing groups to understand each other and form alliances.' Refusing the postmodern formulation of the problem, Hartsock insists that we engage with dominant discourses precisely because we cannot abstract from the complex play of power relations. That wing of postmodernism which holds to the 'vulgar' version of situatedness, cannot engage with the dominant lines of political-economic power at work under capitalism, and thereby typically marginalises itself. This parallels my own conclusion in *The Condition of Postmodernity*:

> while (postmodernism) opens up a radical prospect by acknowledging the authenticity of other voices, postmodernist thinking immediately shuts off those other voices from access to more universal sources of power by ghettoizing them within an opaque otherness, the specificity of this or that language game. It thereby disempowers those voices (of women, ethnic and racial minorities, colonized peoples, the unemployed, youth, etc) in a world of lop-sided power relations. The language game of a cabal of international bankers may be impenetrable to us, but that does not put it on a par with the equally impenetrable language of inner-city blacks from the standpoint of power relations.[35]

By insisting upon mutually exclusionary discourses of the sort to which the narrow definition of situatedness gives rise, we would forcelose upon the most obvious implication of the North Carolina fire: that pursuit of working class politics might protect, rather than oppress and marginalise, interests based on gender and race even if that working class politics regrettably makes no explicit acknowledgement of the importance of race and gender. The failure of a feminist movement strongly implanted within the professions in the United States to respond to events in North Carolina while mobilising around the nomination of a Supreme Court judge, either suggests that narrowly-construed views of situatedness have rather more practical political purchase than many would care to admit or else it tacitly orders situatedness in such a way that what happened to those 'others' in North Carolina was viewed as somehow less important than the nomination of a Supreme Court judge of highly dubious moral standing. They were not necessarily wrong in this for as Haraway points out: it is not *difference* which matters, but *significant* difference:

> In the consciousness of our failures, we risk lapsing into boundless difference and giving up on the confusing task of making partial, real connection. Some differences are playful, some are poles of world historical systems of domination. Epistemology is about knowing the difference.[36]

But what is this 'epistemology' which permits us to know the difference? How should we pursue it? And to what politics does it give rise?

Class Relations, Social Justice and the Politics of Difference

There are a number of disparate threads to be drawn together in the guise of a general conclusion. On the one hand we find a line of argument about social justice that passes through postmodernism and post-structuralism to arrive at a point of recognition that some kind of (unspecified) universals are necessary and that some sort of epistemology (unspecified) is needed to establish when, how and where difference and heterogeneity are significant. On the other hand, we have a political-economic situation, as characterised by the North Carolina deaths, which indicates a seeming paralysis of progressive politics in the face of class oppression. How, then, are we to link the two ends of this theoretical and political tension?

Consider, first, the obvious lesson of the Imperial Foods plant fire: that an effective working class politics would have better protected the rights of men and women, whites and African-Americans in a situation where those particular identities, rather than those of class, were not of primary significance. This conclusion merits embellishment and I will look at it primarily in relation to feminist politics. Lynne Segal has recently noted that 'despite the existence of the largest, most influential and vociferous feminist movement in the world, it is US women who have seen the least *overall* change in the relative disadvantages of their sex, compared to other Western democracies' over the past twenty years.[37] The huge gains made in the United States by women within 'the most prestigious and lucrative professions' have been offset entirely by a life of increasing frustration, impoverishment and powerlessness for the rest. The feminisation of poverty (not foreign to Hamlet, North Carolina) has been, for example, one of the most startling social shifts in the United States over the past two decades, a direct casualty of the Republican-party class-war against the welfare state and working class rights and interests. 'In countries where there have been longer periods of social-democratic government and stronger trade unions,' Segal continues, 'there is far less pay-differential and occupational segregation (both vertical and horizontal) between women and men, and far greater expansion of welfare services.' Given the far superior material conditions of life achieved for women in such social democracies (and I also note parenthetically the savage diminution in many women's rights since 1989 in what was once the communist block), 'it seems strange for feminists to ignore the traditional objectives of socialist or social-democratic parties and organised labour'. It should be noted of course that such institutions have obvious weaknesses and limitations as vehicles for pursuit of feminism's objectives (see, for example, Fraser's compelling argument concerning the gender bias implicit in many welfare state policies).[38] Nevertheless, Segal continues, 'at a time when the advances made by some women are so clearly overshadowed by the increasing poverty experienced so acutely by others (alongside the unemployment of the men of their class and group), it seems perverse to pose women's specific interests *against* rather than *alongside* more traditional socialist goals.' Unless, of course, 'women's interests' are either construed in a very narrow professional and class-biased sense or seen as part of 'an endless game of self-exploration played out on the great board of Identity.'[39]

Segal here parallels Hartsock's concern for the 'bases for political alliances and solidarity.' This requires that we identify 'the *similarities* that can provide the basis for differing groups to understand each other and form alliances.' Young likewise ties the universality criteria she deploys to the idea that 'similarity is never sameness.' Difference can never be characterised, therefore, as 'absolute otherness, a complete absence of relationship or shared attributes.' The *similarity* deployed to measure *difference and otherness* requires, then, just as close an examination (theoretically as well as politically) as does the production of otherness and difference itself. Neither can be established without the other. To discover the basis of similarity (rather than to presume sameness) is to uncover the basis for alliance formation between seemingly disparate groups.

But in today's world, similarity largely resides in that realm of political-economic action so often marginalised in post-structuralist accounts, for it is in terms of commodites, money, market exchange, capital accumulation, and the like that we find ourselves sharing a world of similarity increasingly also characterised by homogeneity and sameness. The radical post-structuralist revolt against that sameness (and its mirror image in some forms of working class politics) has set the tone of recent debates. But the effect has been to throw out the living baby of political and ethical solidarities and similarities across differences, with the cold bathwater of capitalist-imposed conceptions of universality and sameness. Only through critical re-engagement with political-economy, therefore, can we hope to re-establish a conception of social justice as something to be fought for as a key value within an ethics of political solidarity.

Although the conception of justice varies 'not only with time and place, but also with the persons concerned,' we must also here recognise the political force of the fact that a particular conception of it can be 'accepted without misunderstanding' in everyday life. Though 'hopelessly confused' when examined in abstraction, ideals of social justice can still function (as Engels's example of the French Revolution allows) as a powerful mobilising discourse for political action.

But two decades of postmodernism and post-structuralism have left us with little basis to accept any particular norm of social justice 'without misunderstanding', while in everyday life a titanic effort unfolds to convince all and sundry that any kind of regulation of market freedoms or any level of taxation is unjust. Empowerment is then conceived of (as none other than John Major now avows through his active use of the term) as leaving as much money as possible in the wage earners' as well as in the capitalists' pockets; freedom and justice are attached to maximising market choice; and rights are interpreted as a matter of consumer sovereignty free of any government dictates. Perhaps the most important thing missing from the postmodern debate these last two decades is the way in which this right wing and reactionary definition of market justice and of rights has played such a revolutionary role in creating the kind of political economy which produced the effects of the North Carolina fire.

Under such circumstances, reclaiming the terrain of justice and of rights for progressive political purposes appears as an urgent theoretical and political task. But in order to do this we have to come back to that 'epistemology' which helps us tell the difference between significant and non-significant others, differences and situatedness, and which will help promote alliance formation on the basis of similarity rather than sameness. My own epistemology for this purpose rests on a modernised version of historical and geographical materialism, which forms a meta-theoretical framework for examining not only how differences understood as power relations are produced through social action but also how they acquire the particular significance they do in certain situations. From this standpoint it is perfectly reasonable to hold on the one hand, that the philosophical, linguistic and logical critiques of universal propositions about social justice are correct, while acknowledging on the other hand the putative power of appeals to social justice in certain situations, such as the contemporary United States, as a basis for political action. Struggles to bring a particular kind of discourse about justice into a hegemonic position have then to be seen as part of a broader struggle over ideological hegemony between conflicting groups in any society.

Conclusions

The overall effect is to leave us with some important analytical, theoretical and political tasks, which can be summarised as follows:

(1) The universality condition can never be avoided, and those who seek so to do (as is the case in many postmodern and post-structuralist formulations) only end up hiding rather than eliminating the condition. But universality must be construed in dialectical relation with particularity. Each defines the other in such a way as to make the universality criterion always open to negotiation through the particularities of difference. It is useful here to examine the political-economic processes by which society actually achieves such a dialectical unity. Money, for example, possesses universal properties as a measure of value and medium of exchange at the same time as it permits a wide range of highly decentralised and particularistic decision-making in the realm of market behaviours which feed back to define what the universality of money is all about. It is precisely this dialectic which gives strength to right-wing claims concerning individual freedoms and just deserts through market coordinations. While the injustice that derives is plain – the individual appropriation and accumulation of the social power which money represents produces massive and ever widening social inequality – the subtle power of the universality-particularity dialectic at work in the case of money has to be appreciated. The task of progressive politics is to find an equally powerful, dynamic and persuasive way of relating the universal and particular in the drive to define social justice from the standpoint of the oppressed.

(2) Respect for identity and 'otherness' must be tempered by the recognition that though all others may be others, 'some are more other than others' and that in any society certain principles of exclusion have to operate. How this exclusion shall be gauged is embedded in the first instance in a universality condition which prevents groups from imposing their will oppressively on others. This universality condition cannot, however, be imposed

hierarchically from above: it must be open to constant negotiation, precisely because of the way in which disparate claims may be framed (for example, when the rich demand that the oppressive sight (to them) of homelessness be cleared from their vision by expelling the homeless from public spaces).

(3) All propositions for social action (or conceptions of social justice) must be critically evaluated in terms of the situatedness or positionality of the argument and the arguer. But it is equally important to recognise that the individuals developing such situated knowledge are not themselves homogeneous entities but bundles of heterogeneous impulses, many of which derive from an internalisation of 'the other' within the self. Such a conception of the subject renders situatedness itself heterogeneous and differentiated. In the last instance, it is the social construction of situatedness which matters.

(4) The 'espistemology that can tell the difference' between significant and insignificant differences or 'othernesses' is one which can understand the social processes of construction of situatedness, otherness, difference, political identity and the like. And we here arrive at what seems to me to be the most important epistemological point: the relation between social processes of construction of identities on the one hand and the conditions of identity politics on the other. If respect for the condition of the homeless (or the racially or sexually oppressed) does not imply respect for the social processes creating homelessness (or racial or sexual oppression), then identity politics must operate at a dual level. A politics which seeks to eliminate the processes which give rise to a problem looks very different from a politics which merely seeks to give full play to differentiated identities once these have arisen.

We encounter, here a peculiar tension. The identity of the homeless person (or the racially oppressed) is vital to their sense of self-hood. Perpetuation of that sense of self and of identity may depend on perpetuation of the processes which give rise to it. A political programme which successfully combats homelessness (or racism) has to face up to the real difficulty of a loss of identity on the part of those who have been victims of such forms of oppression. And there are subtle ways in which identity, once acquired, can, precisely by virtue of its relative durability, seek out the social conditions (including the oppressions) necessary for its own sustenance.

It then follows that the mere pursuit of identity politics as an end in itself (rather than as a fundamental struggle to break with an identity which internalises oppression) may serve to perpetuate rather than to challenge the persistence of those processes which gave rise to those identities in the first place. This is a pervasive problem even within the ideological debates swirling around identity politics in academia. And it is a problem which is not new, for as Spivak notes of the French post-structuralists:

> (they) forget at their peril that (their) whole overdetermined exercise was in the interest of a dynamic economic situation requiring that interests, motives (desires), and power (of knowledge) be ruthlessly dislocated. To invoke that dislocation now as a radical discovery that should make us diagnose the economic ... as a piece of dated analytic machinery may well be to continue the work of that dislocation and unwittingly to help in securing 'a new balance of hegemonic relations'.[40]

Perhaps this is the best of all possible lessons we can learn from the political failure to respond to events in Hamlet, North Carolina and from the lack of any convincing discourse about social justice with which to confront it. For if the historical and geographical *process* of class-war waged by the Republican Party and the capitalist class these last few years in the United States has feminised poverty, accelerated racial oppression and further degraded the ecological conditions of life, then it seems that a far more united politics can flow from a determination to check *that* process than will likely flow from an identity politics which largely reflects its fragmented results.

Notes

[1] D. Struck, 'South's poultry plants thrive, feeding on workers' need', *Baltimore Sun*, 8.9.91.

[2] O.G. Davidson, 'It's still 1911 in America's rural sweatshops,' *Baltimore Sun*, 7.9.91.

[3] K. Marx, *Capital*, Volume I, International Publishers, New York, 1967.

[4] T. Edsall, *The New Politics of Inequality*, Norton, New York, 1984.

[5] *Ibid*, p 217.

[6] *Ibid*, p 235.

[7] K. Moody, *An Injury to All*, Verso, London, 1988, p 120 and chapter 6.

[8] L. Wittgenstein, *Philosophical Investigations*, Basil Blackwell, Oxford, 1967.

[9] Plato, *The Republic*, Penguin, Harmondsworth, 1965.

[10] K. Marx and F. Engels, *Selected Works*, Volume I, Progess, Moscow, 1951, pp 562-4.

[11] S. White, *Political Theory and Postmodernism*, Cambridge University Press, Cambridge, 1991, p 115-6.

[12] *Ibid*.

[13] K. Marx, *Capital, op cit*, p 235.

[14] M. Walzer, *Spheres of Justice: A defense of pluralism and equality*, Basil Blackwell, Oxford, 1983.

[15] R. Peffer, *Marxism, Morality and Social Justice*, Princeton University Press, Princeton N.J., 1990.

[16] White, *op cit*, p 133.

[17] M. Foucault, *Power/Knowledge*, Harvester-Wheatsheaf, London, 1980, pp 107-8.

[18] J. Lyotard, *The Postmodern Condition*, Manchester University Press, Manchester, 1984.

[19] White, *op cit*, p 107.

[20] See N. Fraser, *Unruly Practices*, University of Minnesota Press, Minneapolis, 1989; and I.M. Young, *Justice and the Politics of Difference*, Princeton University Press, Princeton NJ, 1990(a).

[21] I.M. Young, 'The ideal of community and the politics of difference,' in L. Nicholson (ed), *Feminism/Postmodernism*, Routledge, London, 1990(b) p 312.

[22] *Ibid*, p 321.

[23] Young, 1990a, *op cit*, p 47.

[24] *Ibid*, p 108.

[25] See D. Harvey, 'Between Space and Time, Reflections on the Geographical Imagination', *Annals, Association of American Geographers*, 80, 1990, pp 418-34.

[26] Young 1990a, *op cit*, p 174.

[27] *Ibid*, p 105.

[28] G. Spivak, 'Can the subaltern speak?', in C. Nelson and L. Grossberg (eds), *Marxism and the Interpretation of Culture*, University of Illinois Press, Urbana, 1988.

[29] D. Haraway, 'A Manifesto for Cyborgs: Science, technology and socialist feminism in the 1980s', in L. Nicholson (ed), *Feminism/ Postmodernism*, Routledge, London, 1990; and N. Hartsock, 'Rethinking Modernism: Minority versus majority theories', *Cultural Critique*, 7, 1987, pp 187-206.

[30] Young, *op cit*, p 232.

[31] Spivak, *op cit*, pp 294, 308.

[32] P. Ricoeur, 'Narrative Identity', in D. Wood (ed), *On Paul Ricoeur: Narrative and Interpretation*, Routledge, London, 1991.

[33] H.L. Gates, 'The Welcome Fable: Remembering James Baldwin', Paper delivered to *Wissenschaftliche Jahrestagung der Deutschen Gesellschaft fur Amerikastudien*, Berlin, June, 1992.

[34] Hartsock, *op cit*.

[35] D. Harvey, *The Condition of Postmodernity*, Basil Blackwell, Oxford, 1989, p 117.

[36] Haraway, *op cit*, pp 202-3.

[37] L. Segal, 'Whose Left: Socialism, feminism and the future', New Left Review, 185, 1991, pp 81-91.

[38] Fraser, *op cit*.

[39] Segal, *op cit*, pp 90-91.

[40] Spivak, *op cit*, p 280.

Together in Difference: Transforming the Logic of Group Political Conflict[1]

IRIS MARION YOUNG

William J. Wilson, among others, has forcefully argued that race-focused political movements and policies to improve the lives of poor people of colour are misplaced. Race-focused explanations of black and Hispanic poverty divert attention from the structural changes in the US economy that account primarily for the unemployment and social isolation experienced by rapidly growing numbers of inner city Americans. Race-focused policies such as affirmative action, moreover, have benefited only already better off blacks, and fueled resentment among middle class and working class whites. The problems of poor people, whether white or black, male or female, are best addressed, he argues, through a strong class based analysis of their causes and the promotion of universal public programmes of economic restructuring and redistribution.[2]

Group focused movements and policy proposals, these arguments suggest, only continue resentment and have little chance of success. The more privileged white, male, able-bodied, suburban sectors of this society will not identify with economic and social programmes that they associate with blacks, or women, or Spanish speakers or blind people. Only a broad coalition of Americans uniting behind a programme of universal material benefits to which all citizens have potential access can receive the widespread political support necessary to reverse the 1980s retreat of the state from directing resources to meet needs – programmes such as national health service, family allowance, job training and public works, housing construction and infrastructure revitalisation.

Wilson is at least partly right, both about the causes of poverty and deprivation and the necessity of a broad based coalition of diverse sectors of society coming together to cure them. There are nevertheless basic problems with this approach to political organising and policy. Since the working class, broadly understood, is fractured by relations of privilege and oppression along lines of race, gender, ethnicity, age, ablement, and sexuality, experiential differences and group-based distrust will make it difficult to bring this coalition together unless the distrust is openly addressed and the experiential differences acknowledged. If a unified movement were to develop for a universal working class programme, moreover, it is liable to be led by and reflect the interests of the more privileged segments of each fracture. Wilson's own analysis, for example, is seriously male biased; he tends to perceive female-headed households as pathological, and recommends economic and social programmes that assume women's economic connections to men as the most desirable arrangement. Finally, without countervailing restrictions built in, any universal benefits policies are likely to benefit most those already more privileged. Any new job training programme must learn from the CETA (Central Education and Training Agency) experience, for example, how to combat the tendency to train the already most trainable young white men through programmes that better target young single mothers, older people, and poor people of colour. If a political movement wishes to address the problems of the truly disadvantaged, it must differentiate the needs and experiences of relatively disadvantaged social groups and persuade the relatively privileged – heterosexual men, white people, younger people, the able bodied – to recognise the justice of the group based claims of these oppressed people to specific needs and compensatory benefits. Such recognition should not rule out that a programme for social change benefit these relatively more privileged groups, but justice will be served only if the programmes are designed to benefit the less privileged groups more, and in group specific ways. I believe that some theory and practice of socialist, feminist, black liberation and other group based social movements in the last decade has aimed to develop analysis, rhetoric and political practice along these lines.

I conclude from all this that both a unified working-class based politics and a group differentiated politics are necessary in mobilisations and programmes to undermine oppression and promote social justice in group differentiated societies. Given the above dialectic, however, it is not obvious how both kinds of politics can occur. This problem appears in many forms all over the world; societies, classes, social movements, are riddled with inequality, hatred, competition, and distrust among groups whom necessity brings together politically. This paper examines one aspect of this problem, specifically how political actors conceive group difference and how they might best conceive it. Historically, in group based oppression and conflict difference is conceived as otherness and exclusion, especially, but not only, by hegemonic groups. This conception of otherness relies on a logic of identity that essentialises and substantialises group natures.

Attempts to overcome the oppressions of exclusion which such a conception generates usually move in one of two directions: assimilation or separation. Each of these political strategies itself exhibits a logic of identity; but this makes each strategy contradict the social realities of group interfusion. A third ideal of a single polity with differentiated groups recognising one another's specificity and experience requires a conception of difference expressing a relational rather than substantial logic. Groups should be understood not as entirely other, but as overlapping, as constituted in relation to one another and thus as shifting their attributes and needs in accordance with what relations are salient. In my view, this relational conception of difference as contextual helps make more apparent both the necessity and possibility of political togetherness in difference.

In the second and third sections of this paper I bring this theoretical discussion of difference to bear on interpretations of group based political debate in two contexts outside the United States, which until now has been the focus of my thinking on these issues: group conflict in Eastern Europe and the situation of indigenous people in New Zealand.

Group conflict in Eastern Europe appears fairly intractable, with group differentiated unities disintegrating rather than forming. Separatisms have emerged there that exhibit essentialist constructions of group identity and define difference as otherness. Yet social realities dictate the necessary interdependence and interspersion of these groups. In many places in Eastern Europe the tragedy appears to be that group differentiated single polities are necessary, but group exclusions render them impossible.

Recent public debate about the political status of the indigenous Maori people projects more hope for the emergence of a heterogeneous public. Some of the Maori advocates have expressed an ideal of political biculturalism against the more assimilationist rhetoric of the dominant white officials and popular politicians. The Maori movement has succeeded to a certain extent in shifting political rhetoric and policy from this assimilationist position to one that recognises biculturalism in some respects.

Group Difference as Otherness

Social groups who identify one another as different typically have conceived that difference as Otherness. Where the social relation of the groups is one of privilege and oppression, this attribution of Otherness is asymmetrical. While the privileged group is defined as active human subject, inferiorised social groups are objectified, substantialised, reduced to a nature or essence.[3] Whereas the privileged groups are neutral, exhibit free, spontaneous and weighty subjectivity, the dominated groups are marked with an essence, imprisoned in a given set of possibilities. By virtue of the characteristics the dominated group is alleged to have by nature, the dominant ideologies allege that those group members have specific dispositions that suit them for some activities and not others. Using its own values, experience, and culture as standards, the dominant group measures the Others and finds them essentially lacking, as excluded from and/or complementary to themselves. Group difference as otherness thus usually generates dichotomies of mind and body, reason-emotion, civilized and primitive, developed and underdeveloped.

Gender is a paradigm of this presumption that difference is otherness. Gender categorisation of biological and social group differences between men and women typically makes them mutually exclusive complementary opposites. Western culture, and other cultures as well, systematically classify many behaviours and attributes according to mutually exclusive gender categories that lie on a superior-inferior hierarchy modeled on a mind-body dichotomy. Men are rational, women emotional, men are rule-bound contractors, women are caretakers, men are right-brainers, women are left-brainers. Dichotomous essentialising gender ideologies have traditionally helped legitimate women's exclusion from privileged male places.

The oppressions of racism and colonialism operate according to similar oppositions and exclusions. The privileged and dominating group defines its own positive worth by negatively valuing the Others and projecting onto them as an essence or nature the attributes of evil, filth, bodily matter; these oppositions legitimate the dehumanised use of the despised group as sweated labour and domestic servants, while the dominant group reserves for itself the leisure, refined surroundings, and high culture that mark civilisation.[4]

Not all social situations of group difference have such

extremely hierarchical relations of privilege and oppression. Sometimes groups are more equal than this model portrays, even though they may not be equal in every respect. Nevertheless, many such situations of group difference and conflict rely on a conception of difference as Otherness. Some of the conflicting groups in Eastern Europe seem roughly equal in this way and nevertheless see their relation as one of mutual exclusion. I will return to this later.

Whether unequal or relatively equal, difference as otherness conceives social groups as mutually exclusive, categorically opposed. This conception means that each group has its own nature and shares no attributes with those defined as other. The ideology of group difference in this logic attempts to make clear borders between groups, and to identify the characteristics that mark the purity of one group off from the characteristics of the Others.

This conception of group difference as Otherness exhibits a logic of identity. Postmodern critiques of the logic of identity argue that much Western thought denies or represses difference, which is to say, represses the particularity and heterogeneity of sensual experience and the everyday language immersed in it. Rational totalising thought reduces heterogeneity to unity by bringing the particulars under comprehensive categories. Beneath these linguistic categories, totalising thought posits more real substances, self-same entities underlying the apparent flux of experience. These substances firmly fix what does and does not belong within the category, what the thing is and is not. This logic of identity thereby generates dichotomy rather than unity, dichotomies of what is included and what is excluded from the categories. Through this dialectic initial everyday experience of particular differences and variations among things and events become polarised into mutually exclusive oppositions: light-dark, air-earth, mind-body, public-private, and so on. Usually the unifying discourse imposes a hierarchical valuation on these dichotomies, lining them up with a good-bad dichotomy.

The method of deconstruction shows how categories which the logic of identity projects as mutually exclusive in fact depend on one another. The essence of the more highly valued or 'pure' side of a dichotomy usually must be defined by reference to the very category to which it is opposed. Deconstructive criticism demonstrates how essentialised categories are constructed by their relations with one another, and bursts the claim that they correspond to a purely present reality. Deconstruction not only exposes the meaning of categories as contextual, but also reveals their differentiation from others as undecidable: the attempt to demarcate clear and permanent boundaries between things or concepts will always founder on the shifts in context, purpose and experience that change the relationships or the perspectives describing them. Allegedly fixed identities thus melt down into differentiated relations.

Defining groups as Other actually denies or represses the heterogeneity of social difference, understood as variation and contextually experienced relations. It denies the difference among those who understand themselves as belonging to the same group; it reduces the members of the group to a set of common attributes. Insofar as the group categorisation takes one set of attributes as a standard in reference to which it measures the nature of other groups as complementary, lacking, excluded, moreover, it robs the definition of a group's attributes of its own specificity.

The method of deconstruction shows how a self-present identity – whether posited as a thing, a substantial totality, a theoretical system, or a self – drags shadows and traces that spill over that unity, which the discourse representing the identity represses at the same time that it relies on them for its meaning. This process of criticism that reveals the traces, exhibits the failure of discourse to maintain a pure identity, because it appears as internally related to what it claims to exclude. Attempts to posit solid and pure group identities in social life fail in just this way. The practical realities of social life, especially but not only in modern, mass, economically interdependent societies, defy the attempt to conceive and enforce group difference as exclusive opposition. Whatever the group opposition, there are always ambiguous persons who do not fit the categories. Modern processes of urbanisation and market economy produce economic interdependencies, the physical intermingling of members of differently identifying groups in public places and workplaces, and partial identities cutting across more encompassing group identities.

Think, for example, of the social disruptions of an oppositional gender dichotomy. Homosexuality is the most obvious problem here. Enforced heterosexuality is a cornerstone of the gender edifice that posits exclusive opposition between masculine and feminine. The essence of man is to 'have' woman and the essence of women is to depend on and reflect man. Men who love men and women who love women disrupt this system along many axes, proving by their deeds that even this most 'natural' of differences blurs and breaks down.[5] Thus the need to make homosexuality invisible is at least as much existential and ontological as it is moral.

The inability to maintain categorical opposition between social groups appears in examining any social group difference, however. Where there are racial, ethnic, or national group differences there is always the 'problem' of those who do not fit because they are of 'mixed' parentage. The effort to divide such racial or ethnic groups by territory is always thwarted by what to do with those frontier areas where opposing groups mingle residentially, or how to account for and reverse the fact that members of one group reside as a minority population in a neighbourhood, city or territory conceptually or legally dominated by another. The needs of capital for cheap labour increasingly exacerbate this problem of the 'out groups' dwelling in the territory from which they are conceptually excluded. Capital encourages despised or devalued groups defined as Other to accept low paying menial jobs which keep them excluded from the privileges of the dominant group, but cannot keep them physically excluded from land and buildings the privileged claim as theirs. In many parts of the world those defined as 'guest workers' have become a permanent presence, and survive as blatantly ambiguous groups, excluded by definition from the places where they live, but excluded as well from their supposed homelands.[6]

The method of deconstruction consists in showing how one term in a binary opposition internally relates to the other. Group difference conceived as Otherness exhibits a similar dialectic. Frequently the most vociferous xenophobia, homophobia, misogyny arises as a result of a logic that defines a self-identity primarily by its negative relation to the Other. Some gender theorists suggest, for example, that for many men masculinity is primarily defined as what women are not.[7] Racist discourses similarly articulate the purity and virtue of white civilization by detailed fascinated attention to the attributes of the coloured Others, and the white subjects thereby derive their sense of identity from this negative relation to the Other. A group identity formed as a negation of the Other in these ways is fragile and relatively empty, and perhaps for that reason often violently insists on maintaining the purity of its border by excluding that Other.[8] This negative dialectic of group identity denies the subjects so identified a positive specificity. If men were less worried about avoiding invasion by feminine attributes, they might better be able to consider whether there is anything positively specific about masculine experience that does not depend on excluding, devaluing and dominating women.

To challenge this conceptualisation of difference as otherness and exclusive opposition, I propose a conception of difference that better recognises heterogeneity and interspersion of groups. It makes explicit the relational logic I just articulated according to which even the most fixed group identities define themselves in relation to others. A more fluid, explicitly relational conception of difference need not repress the interdependence of groups in order to construct a substantial conception of group identity.[9]

This relational conception of difference does not posit a social group as having an essential nature composed of a set of attributes defining only that group. Rather, a social group exists and is defined as a specific group only in social and interactive relation to others. Social group identities emerge from the encounter and interaction among people who experience some differences in their way of life and forms of association, even if they regard themselves as belonging to the same society. So a group exists and is defined as a specific group only in social and interactive relation to others. Group identity is not a set of objective facts, but the product of experienced meanings.

In this conception difference does not mean otherness, or exclusive opposition, but rather specificity, variation, heterogeneity. Difference names relations of both similarity and dissimilarity that can be reduced neither to coextensive identity nor overlapping otherness. Different groups always potentially share some attributes, experiences, or goals. Their differences will be more or less salient depending on the groups compared and the purposes of the comparison. The characteristics that make one group specific and the borders that distinguish it from other groups are always *undecidable*.

A primary virtue of this altered conception of group difference is that from it we can derive a social and political ideal of togetherness in difference which I think best corresponds to the political needs of most contemporary situations of group based injustice and conflict. Continuing my previous work on this theme, I will call this the ideal of a heterogeneous public.[10] Perhaps the best way to explore the uniqueness of this ideal is to contrast it with the two ideals that tend to surface in contemporary political debate and strategies involving group oppression or group conflict: assimilation and separation.

The tradition of liberal individualism promotes an assimilationist ideal. It condemns group based exclusions and discriminations, along with the essentialist ideologies of group superiority and objectification that legitimate these oppressions. Liberal individualism not only rightly calls these conceptions of group identity and difference into question, it also claims that social group categorisations are invidious fictions whose sole function is to justify privilege. In fact there are no significant categorical group based differences among persons, this position suggests. People should be considered as individuals only, and not as members of groups. They should be evaluated on their individual merits and treated in accordance with their actions and achievements, not according to ascribed characteristics or group affinities which they have not chosen.

Liberal individualism thus proposes an assimilationist ideal as a political goal. The assimilationist ideal envisions a society where a person's social group membership, physical attributes, genealogy, and so on, make no difference for their social position, the advantages or disadvantages that accrue to them, or how other people relate to them. Law and other rules of formal institutions will make no distinction among persons and will assume their moral and political equality. In a society which has realized this assimilationist ideal, people might retain certain elements of group identity, such as religious affiliation or ethnic association. But such group affiliation would be completely voluntary, and a purely private matter. It would have no visible expression in the institutional structure of the society. Workplaces, political institutions, and other public arenas would presume every person as the same, which is to say a free self-making individual.[11]

The assimilationist ideal properly rejects any conception of group difference as otherness, exclusive opposition, and rightly seeks individual freedom, equality and self-development. It wrongly believes, however, that the essentialist substantialising conception of group identity and difference is the only conception. The liberal individualist position associates group based oppression with assertions of group differences as such; eliminating group oppression such as racism, then, implies eliminating group differences.

There are several problems with this assimilationist ideal. First, it does not correspond to experience. Many people who are oppressed or disadvantaged because of their group identity nevertheless find significant sources of personal friendship, social solidarity, and aesthetic satisfaction in their group based affinities and cultural life. While the objectifying, fixed conception of group identity is false, it does not follow that group identity is false altogether. Some group affinities that mean a great deal to people are not tied to privilege and oppression; even among presently privileged groups one can find positive group affinity networks and culturally specific styles that help define people's sense of themselves without being tied to the oppression or exclusion of others. The assimilationist ideal exhibits a logic of identity by denying group difference and positing all persons as interchangeable from a moral and political point of view.

Second, the assimilationist ideal also presumes a conception of the individual self as transcending or prior to social context. As Sandel and others have argued, however, a conception of the self as socially constituted and embedded in particular communities is much more reasonable.[12] The assimilationist ideal carries an implicit normative requirement that the authentic self is one that has voluntarily assumed all aspects of her or his life and identity. Such a voluntarist conception of self is unrealistic, undesirable, and unnecessary. We cannot say that someone experiences injustice or coercion simply by finding themselves in social relationships they have not chosen. If unchosen relationships do not produce systematic group inequality and oppression, and also allow individuals considerable personal liberty of action, then they are not unjust.

The strategy for undermining group based oppression implied by the assimilationist ideal, finally, is not likely to succeed under circumstances where there are cultural differences among groups and some groups are privileged. If particular gender, racial or ethnic groups have greater economic, political or social power, their group related experiences, points of view, or cultural assumptions will tend to become the norm, biasing the standards or procedures of achievement and inclusion that govern social, political and economic institutions. To the degree that the dominant culture harbours prejudices or stereotypes about the disadvantaged groups, moreover, these are likely to surface in awarding positions or benefits, even when the procedures claim to be colour-blind, gender-blind, or ethnically neutral. Behaviourally or linguistically based tests and evaluations cannot be culturally neutral, moreover, because behaviours and language cannot be. When oppressed or disadvantaged social groups are different from dominant groups, then, an allegedly group-neutral assimilationist strategy of inclusion only tends to perpetuate inequality.[13]

Contemporary oppressed or disadvantaged social groups with these criticisms of an assimilationist strategy have often envisioned only one alternative to it, the separatist strategy. Understood in its purist form, separatism says that freedom and self-development for an oppressed or disadvantaged group will best be enacted if that group separates from the dominant society, and establishes political, economic and social autonomy. For many separatist movements this vision implies the establishment of a separate sovereign state with a distinct and contiguous territory. Some movements of cultural minorities and oppressed groups, especially those with residentially dispersed populations, do not find such a state feasible. Radical separatist policies nevertheless call for maintaining and establishing group based political, cultural, and especially economic institutions through which members of the group can pursue a good life as much as possible independently of other groups.

I think that the separatist impulse is an important aspect of any movement of oppressed or disadvantaged groups in a society. It helps establish cultural autonomy and political solidarity among members of the group. By forcing dominant groups who have assumed themselves as neutral and beneficent to experience rejection, moreover, separatism also often threatens and disturbs dominant powers more than other political stances. Sometimes the separatist impulse results in the construction of institutions and practices that do make life better for the oppressed or disadvantaged group, and/or give it more political leverage with which to confront dominant groups.

A separatist inspired philosophy of 'women helping women' has established rape crisis centres and battered women's shelters in North America, for example, or women-based economic co-operatives in places such as Chile or India (though in the latter cases the organisers may not call themselves feminist separatists).

Separatism asserted by oppressed groups is very different from the processes of enforced separation, segregation and exclusion perpetrated by dominating groups that assert their superiority. Dominant groups depend for their sense of identity on defining the excluded group as Other and keeping the border between themselves and the Other clear. Separatism is inward looking where chauvinism looks outward; separatism is a positive self-assertion where racism and anti-Semitism are negative; separation of the oppressed is voluntary where their exclusion is coerced. Nevertheless, separatism also submits to a logic of identity structurally akin to that underlying a conception of difference as Otherness. It aims to purify and enclose a group identity and thereby avoid political conflict with other groups.

The aim of self-determination and autonomy propelling separatist movements might be sensible if it were not the case that almost everywhere the groups in conflict are already together, their histories intertwined with mutual influences as well as antagonisms. As I discussed earlier, most social groups today currently reside in patterns interspersed with other groups; where the groups are relatively segregated geographically, there are usually mixed border areas, or some members of a relatively separated group are dispersed elsewhere. Groups that perceive themselves as very different in one context, moreover, often find themselves similar when they together encounter another group. But most important, processes of economic centralisation and diversification, along with urbanisation, have created a necessary economic interdependence among many groups and regions that would much prefer to be separate.

The logic of identity expressed by separatist assertions and movements, finally, often tends to simplify and freeze the identity of its group in a way that fails to acknowledge the group differences within a social group. A strong nationalist separatist movement, for example, may reinforce or increase its domination of women or a religious minority, because it wrongly essentialises and homogenises the attributes of members of the group.

I conclude from these arguments that social movements of oppressed or disadvantaged groups need a political vision different from both the assimilationist and separatist ideals. I derive such a vision from the relational conception of group difference. A politics that treats difference as variation and specificity, rather than as exclusive opposition, aims for a society and polity where there is social equality among explicitly differentiated groups who conceive themselves as dwelling together without exclusions.

What are the elements of such an ideal? First, the groups in question understand themselves as participating in the same society. Whether they like ir or not, they move within social processes that involve considerable exchange, interaction, and interdependency among the groups. Their being together may produce conflicts, division, relations of privilege and oppression that motivate their *political* interaction.

Thus, second, to resolve these conflicts the group must be part of a single polity. The polity should foster institutions and procedures for discussing and deciding policies that all can accept as legitimately binding, thereby creating a public in which the groups communicate.

But, third, this public is *heterogeneous*, which means that the social groups of the society have a differentiated place in that public, with mutual recognition of the specificity of the groups in the public. Political processes of discussion and decision-making provide for the specific representation of those groups in the society who are oppressed or disadvantaged, because a more universal system of representation is unlikely to include them in manner or numbers sufficient to grant their perspective political influence. The primary moral ground for this heterogeneous public is to promote social justice in its policies.

Besides guaranteeing individual civil and political rights, and guaranteeing that the basic needs of individuals will be met so that they can freely pursue their own goals, a vision of social justice provides for some group related rights and policies. These group institutions will adhere to a principle that social policy should attend to rather than be blind to group difference in awarding benefits or burdens, in order to remedy group based inequality or meet group specific needs.

Group Conflict in Eastern Europe[14]

Scores of group identities pepper what were recently the eight nation-states of Eastern Europe: the Soviet Union, Poland, Czechoslovakia, Hungary, Yugoslavia, Romania, Bulgaria, and Albania. A history of movement, migration, empires, and wars in this region of the world has resulted in a dispersion of many self-identifying groups in several places, not always contiguous. Few places on this earth have escaped such a general process, although the specific histories, of course, vary widely. One group is often dispersed among several of the existing states. Many self-identified nationalities have never had a state in the modern institutional sense. Despite mythologies of pure ethnicities with unitary homelands, virtually every territory has its ethnic and often religious minorities.

With the receding of Communism in this region ethnopolitics has burst on the scene with such passion and violence that it is difficult not to interpret it as a 'return of the repressed'. The policies and practices of the Communist states claimed to have made relations among these groups orderly and co-operative, but this is primarily because limited political freedom repressed some group conflict and claims to autonomy.

The philosophy and policies of these Communist states have certainly had assimilationist tendencies, deriving at least in part from Marxism itself. The Marxist tradition shares with liberalism a modernist Englightenment orientation which regards ascribed statuses and traditional group based affiliations as conservatising, divisive, and irrational. Historical materialism's theory of social evolution theorises that capitalist development breaks down such status-based social power and distinction, and brings diverse groupings together as workers. The more universal relationships of bourgeois and proletariat emerge, which transcend national, regional and ethnic boundaries. The socialist movement of the nineteenth century was vigorously internationalist, based on this philosophy. Its vision of the future socialist society implied the creation for the first time of a truly universal humanity, not divided by arbitrary boundaries of state, nation or ethne.

In applying the international socialist vision to the concrete context of Eastern Europe, the Bolshevik revolution had to modify this universalist vision. In so doing, the early Russian revolution developed some theory and practice for a state's relation with national minorities that exhibited more sensitivity and progressive tendency than many other places in the world. After World War Two several instances of really existing socialism claimed to have constitutional federations that guaranteed cultural pluralism. There is some reason to think, however, that Communist philosophy regarded such cultural pluralism as a necessary accommodation to existing conditions, and that ethnic affiliation would wither away within the worker's state. Thus Philip Roeder argues, for example, that Soviet Federalism aimed toward assimilation in the long run, even though it accorded special rights to national groups.[15] Yugoslav federalism before the 1970s, to take another example, concretely exemplified the impulse to create a socialist identity that would merge and transcend traditional ethnic identities.

Assimilationist tendencies in Eastern Europe in the last forty years may also be partly attributed to the policies of the major allied powers at the end of World War Two. According to Jonathan Eyal, after 1945 Britain, France and the United States looked at cultural minorities in Eastern Europe and

concluded that if all citizens were allowed to enjoy their

civil rights irrespective of race, language or creed, all would be well. But these were essentially excuses, for both Britain and France entertained few illusions about the future of 'democracy' in Eastern Europe. Rather, they feared that an international system of minorities protection would apply to the West as well as to the East, and they were determined to prevent this from happening.[16]

Against this history of what they perceive either as minority repression or co-optive granting of superficial group rights, many national and ethnic groups have won, and more are demanding, separation from the state jurisdictions in which they have been lodged for more than forty years, and the establishment of their own sovereign polities. Often this separatism has produced its own unifying and repressive consequences, as other ethnic minorities within the territories for which a nationality claims separate sovereignty find themselves excluded from full citizenship recognition and economic opportunity. Ethnic Russians in Lithuania, for example, experience disadvantage and discrimination in the context of Lithunian separatism. In Latvia, ethnic Russians make up a large part of the population, while Latvians account for just over fifty per cent of the inhabitants.[17]

The causes of the terrible wars in Croatia and Bosnia-Herzegovina are clearly multiple and overdetermined, not least of them involving power jockeying and the loss of central government civilian control over the Yugoslav army. But a vociferous notion of difference as Otherness appears to be among these causes. Nationalist movements aim to define a Croat or Serb or Montenegran identity in whole and essential terms, as pure and coherent, and entirely other than that of its neighbours. The groups often tell stories of origins, of the group in its primeval purity, and attach those origins to an original place, from which they now conceive themselves as displaced, or into which others have invaded and do not primordially belong.

Language, national symbols, cultural artifacts such as dress and texts, and above all this constructed primordial history give to the group its essence, which is unique, timeless and unshared by any other group. Where some people outside their region might find the groups nearly indistinguishable, they tend to deny any similarities. The groups from which the group distinguishes itself in order to form its identity come to be constructed as evil Others, all members of the Other group also essentially the same. Because some Croats were fascists and committed genocide during World War Two, in the minds of nationalist Serbs all Croats become natural fascists.

The history of the movement of peoples and the cultural influence and economic interdependence of the peoples of this region seem to me to exemplify the importance of a fluid and relational conception of group difference, which understands groups as overlapping, criss-crossing, and with undecidable borders. Every former Yugoslav Republic has several differently identifying groups within its territory, among which there has been considerable intermarriage, friendship, mutual interaction and influence. The interfusion among groups is profound, which sets the conditions for violent genocide once they, or some of them, decide that they are separate and unique, requiring a separate and homogeneous state and territory.

Thus several of the new constitutions of the former Yugoslav republics, including Croatia and Macedonia, attempt to define the essence of the national identity into their constitutions. According to Robert M. Hayden:

> Constitutional Nationalism both establishes and attempts to protect the constitution of that national as a bounded entity: a sovereign being with its own defining language, culture and perhaps 'biological being', the uniqueness of which must be defended at any cost ... The cultural concomitants of national identity are also being increasingly viewed as bounded, determinate structures of language, belief, religion, practice. In a return to an old European concatenation, a given nation is seen as having a single, language, a single culture, a single heritage, a single interest.[18]

In these societies where so recently many people had a

weak sense of group identity, today in such republics people are forced to locate themselves in one and only one group, having to face serious exclusions if they are not in the nationally dominant group. Such unique and pure identification is tragically impossible for the many people who have married across these boundaries, and for their children. According to Hayden, even in the most homogeneous of the republics, Slovenia, only 73 per cent of the children listed on the 1981 census issues from 'ethnically pure' Slovenian marriages, while in the most bitterly contested areas of Croatia as many as 35 per cent of the children were from mixed Serb-Croat marriages.

In reaction to the assimilationist tendencies they associate with the former Yugoslav Communist state, many of these nationalist groups are asserting a militant separatism, which claims the need for a separate national territory and also claims to include ethnic minorities located in other territories. This separatism raises well grounded fears on the part of national minorities within a national state, who in turn call for their own separate territory. But nowhere is there any territory that contains only one national group. Thus the spiral of separation that breeds more efforts at separation generates only increased hostility. In this region, where the interfusion of groups is so complete and borders of their difference so undecidable, it appears that only forced removal and genocide can homogenise a territory.

The situation of ethnic Albanians in the Serbian province of Kosovo, and the dispute about their status, appears to be typical of many ethnic disputes in the region along the dimensions I have been discussing. Many fear that this conflict will prompt the next war, probably involving several countries in the region. Since the early 1980s, the ethnic Albanians who compose an increasing majority of the province of Kosovo have asserted a separatist claim. They wish to have a separate republic in Yugoslavia, with the same political status as the other six republics. Ethnic Albanians claim that their current status as a province within Serbia has put them at the mercy of Serbian hegemony and hatred. They claim that the

Yugoslav and Serbian governments have failed to invest in productive industry in Kosovo, and have instead pursued a development strategy based on extracting raw materials from the province to be used for industrial development elsewhere. Serbs and Montenegrins are favoured by the government in the distribution of public housing in the province, and they hold government office in numbers out of proportion to their numbers in the general population of Kosovo, which together is less than 10 per cent. The Serbian government has systematically repressed expression of Albanian national and cultural experience and symbols, they claim, for most of the last five decades. While these assimilationist policies were relaxed somewhat in the 1970s, the establishment by the Serbian government of a state of emergency in the 1980s has redoubled the oppression of ethnic Albanians.[19]

The Serbs tell a rather different story. Kosovo, they assert, is their original homeland, which those now called Albanians invaded in the seventeenth century. Collaborators with the Italian fascists during the 1930s and 40s, the ethnic Albanians in Kosovo persecuted and killed the Serbs and Montenegrins. Since World War Two, and especially since the early 1980s, Albanians have suppressed non-Albanian cultural expression, destroyed churches, and created such hardship for Serbs and Montenegrins that tens of thousands have left their homes in Kosovo for neighbouring provinces and republics. The government of Serbia, they claim, has been most generous in its support for Albanian cultural and economic maintenance.[20] As far as I can gather from this distance, the Albanians legitimately claim to be oppressed in Serbia, though there is no excuse for retaliatory violence against Serbs in Kosovo.

I believe that most of the group social movements in Eastern Europe currently protesting their state's policies, engaging in conflicts with other groups, and/or establishing separate states, have claims of justice that deserve a hearing among those with whom they are thrown together or with whom they find themselves in conflict. Separation, involving the establishment of new sovereign jurisdictions, does not offer much of a solution to these problems of privilege, oppression and conflict.

Because of the interfusion of groups in the same territories and multiple group claims over many territories, some groups are harmed no matter how the borders are drawn. As separatist national movements aim to break off their autonomous territory from the larger states of the Soviet Union or Yugoslavia, new minorities within those smaller jurisdictions are inevitably created. The idea of any ethnic or nationally 'pure' polity is a chimera, moreover, and those who see in it ghosts of Nazism have grounds for their fears. The economies of Eastern Europe, finally, are so interdependent that self-sufficiency for any region is a near impossibility. This social and economic interfusion of groups in Eastern Europe implies that they must dwell together in tight political relations, whether they want to or not. Establishing new legal borders and sovereign territories perhaps shifts bargaining power within those relations, but it cannot politically separate the parties. The immediate creation of a new federation of nations of the now independent states that were formerly the Soviet Union attests to the necessity of their remaining together in their difference.

Some commentators appear to draw the conclusion from these horrible conflicts that only a liberal individualist conception of the polity is legitimate. The mistake is to give groups any political recognition at all. People should look on themselves as individuals, simply human begins, and should look on others this way as well. The degree of attachment that people have to group identities makes such a response utopian. As I discussed earlier, it presumes an abstract and voluntarist conception of the self. The only hope for political co-operation, peace and justice in this region, it seems to me, lies in establishing or re-establishing layers of heterogeneous publics that guarantee respect for the cultural specificity and needs of different groups, and which compensate disadvantaged groups, institutionalising means of ensuring that their voice and perspective will be heard. At the time of writing, the principals in the awful war in Bosnia-Herzegovina are conducting talks on a constitutional proposal which perhaps goes a little way toward calling for such a heterogeneously federated polity. Since it is still premised on the separate identities of groups in separate territories, however, it is unlikely to bring a stable peace.

The Maori Movement in New Zealand

During the 1970s and 1980s New Zealand society debated the status of Maori people as a result of a concerted Maori social movement. As described by Andrew Sharp in *Justice and the Maori*, this political debate, by no means over, succeeded at some level in creating a heterogeneous public. Initially, liberal individualist assimilationalist arguments dominated the debate. The Maori movement rejected these arguments, and some of them organised a separatist party. What resulted from the debate, according to Sharp, was the recognition of Maori distinctness within the New Zealand polity and society.

> Although the tension between unity and difference was always likely to be resolved in a way which denied justice to the Maori people (by insisting on seeing them as so many separate individuals who were part of the New Zealand nation), yet they persisted in, and won, a propaganda battle with politicians over their separateness. Perhaps this is the best that can be said of the history of the conflicts of the 1970s and 1980s, with respect to justice.[21]

People of Maori descent (as well as Pacific Islands) suffer disadvantage in New Zealand society along a great many measurable dimensions. Only about ten per cent of the total population, Maori have next to no political influence, even though Parliament seats have been reserved for them for decades. They are outvoted and outnumbered in most areas of common social life, where the dominant European interests and perspectives hold sway *de facto*. In areas of income, longevity, access to health care, housing, education, employment, Maoris fall short compared with whites. Proportionately more Maori than whites are in prison, suffer police abuse, and in general come into contact with law enforcement authorities. Like most indigenous peoples in most other parts of the world, the Maori suffer employment discrimination, and they occupy proportionately fewer professional positions in the society than whites.

Before colonial contact there had been no 'Maori' group; there were only individual tribes and village groups. A self-identified Maori people has formed only in the context of confrontation with and differentiation from the European settlers. In 1840 several tribal chiefs signed a Treaty at Waitangi which represented the indigenous people in an agreement with the British crown. Like other European colonial treaties with indigenous peoples, the Treaty of Waitangi recognised the Maori as a distinct people, and promised to reserve land and fishing and hunting rights for them. In return the Maori promised to recognise Crown claims to sovereignty over most of the Aoetorian lands. Like most other such treaties in the rest of the world, the Europeans did not keep their end of the bargain and the Maori had no choice but to keep theirs.

A Maori identity emerged from this encounter with Europeans (called Pakeha by Maori) with very different language, culture, customs and values. This illustrates the idea that social group difference is best described as relational, rather than defined by essences and common attributes. Sharp notes,

> The truth is that the Maori-Pakeha distinction of people and culture is, like any other distinction between groups of people, made, constructed, fashioned from a world of perceptions of similarity and difference which is far more complex than the distinction can express. (p 51)

Sharp also points out that at least at the beginning of the current debate in New Zealand, there was no distinct 'European' identity, no self-conscious pride in European based (primarily British) tradition, no conception of the encounter with the Maori revealing the specificity and relativity of their colonial culture. More often the Europeans viewed the Maori as deviant – backward, uncivilized – from an allegedly culturally neutral set of standards of progress, efficiency, rationality, etc. Many white New Zealanders denied that a group difference between Maori and whites existed any longer. They claimed that generations of living together had made them one nation of New Zealanders, and that in New Zealand people are and should be thought of as individuals, not as members of groups.

In their politicised assertion of positive group difference beginning in the 70s, the Maori vociferously denied this assimilationist picture, but it did have an element of truth that illustrates my point about undecidability in group difference. For while it was and remains possible to say that Maori and Pakeha are different social groups, 'the realities of biological, social and cultural mixing between Maori and Pakeha and their ways of life made a clear distinction between them impossible (p 46).

The Maori asserted that New Zealand politics and society should acknowledge them as a distinct people with a distinct language, culture and way of life. They claimed that because of generations of domination by the Pakeha people they deserved reparations, and they asserted the need for redistribution of New Zealand's resources to provide the Maori with a greater share. They asserted the right to speak their own language in official settings, to administer their own lands and fisheries and to a distinct legal system. They included other planks in the platform for Maori improvement and self-determination, including affirmative action in education and employment, state subsidisation of Maori business and economic development.

Many whites reacted to these assertions of Maori specificity with a liberal individualist response. The political institutions of modern representative democracy do not or should not differentiate citizens. All persons, whatever their social or cultural background, should be considered equal before the law. Law and state policy should be blind to differences of ethnicity or origin, and promote the ability of each individual to achieve whatever they be in competition with others. If those of Maori origin have been disadvantaged and discriminated against, then steps should be taken to remove the barriers to their full inclusion in New Zealand society. But such steps cannot include special recognition for Maori culture and group economy, because that will only continue to keep them marked and disadvantaged. The Maori responded to this reasonable liberalism by claiming that its assimilationist point of view perpetuated cultural imperialism.

> Inequalities were the outcome of monocultural institutions which simply ignore or freeze out the cultures of those who do not belong to the majority. National cultures are evolved which are rooted in the values, systems and viewpoints of one culture only. Participation by minorities is conditional on their subjugating their own values and systems to those of 'the system' of the power culture. The aim should be to attain socio-economic parity between Maori and non-Maori by the provision of resources to meet Maori needs on Maori terms. (p 212)

Separatism was one challenge to the dominant assimilationist position. In 1979 a former minister of Maori Affairs led the founding of a separatist Maori party, which was an important player in the debate. Separatists called for political separation of Maori and Pakeha, with complete Maori sovereignty over Maori lives, land, and fisheries. Perhaps because no single territory could be conceived as the Maori 'homeland', however, and because most Maori are thoroughly interspersed in New Zealand society, with the majority living in cities, complete separation could not be understood as a serious option.

A more realistic Maori political ideal emerged in the doctrine of biculturalism. As defined by Sharp, bicultu-ralism 'was the doctrine that distributions of things in Aoteraroa/New Zealand should be made primarily between the two main cultures, Maori and Pakeha, and that since Maori and Pakeha were *ethne* worthy of equal respect, the distributions should be equal between them (p 227). Given the power of the Pakeha and the relatively small numbers of Maori, the idea of an equal distribution of political and economic power between the two groups met with insurmountable resistance. Nevertheless, by the late 1980s a general principle of biculturalism was recognised by many people, and institutionalised to some extent in law. The Royal Commission on the electoral system, for example, recommended a multiple member proportional representational system. It also urged that procedures for elections to Hospital Boards, University Councils, City Councils, and Parliament be so modified that Maori representatives might be chosen according to the custom of the Maori themselves (pp 237, 243). Legislation has been enacted which prohibits passage of any bill which is regarded as inconsistent with Maori land holdings. Government reform to recognise biculturalism and give Maori special rights of control over Maori affairs extended beyond legislation, moreover, to the organisation of government bureaucracy.[22]

The debate in New Zealand about what a bicultural society and polity with special rights for the Maori means has not ended, and perhaps cannot end. Specific conflicts of interest between the groups will continue to surface. Disagreements and resentments continue among both groups. Sharp indicates that he believes that the Maori have not yet received justice, especially economic justice. Nevertheless, as I read Sharp's story, the political debate and institutional changes of the 1980s established a heterogeneous public which provides some institutionalised group specific voice for the disadvantaged group and asserts a principle of special rights for the sake of preserving the group's culture and way of life.

Conclusion

I began this paper by referring to a dilemma faced by those seeking change in social policy in the United States toward economic restructing that will be oriented to meeting needs. The dilemma appears to be that a unified class-based social movement is necessary to achieve this change, on the one hand, but justice within and as a result of such a movement requires differentiating group needs and perspectives and fostering respect for those differences, on the other. My analyses of Eastern Europe and New Zealand are partly designed to demonstrate that this sort of dilemma is hardly unique to the context of the United States. All over the world group based claims to special rights, to cultural justice and the importance of recognising publicly different group experiences and perspectives have exploded, often with violence.

In many places the claims, debates and conflicts of this ethnopolitics seem to dwarf other political issues. When they do it is generally no less true there than in the United States that economic structures are a primary case of group disadvantage, where it exists. Some socialists, and some liberals as well, might rightly claim that focus on political group difference and conflict diverts attention from these issues of economic structure.

In this paper I have suggested that the context of economic interdependence provides an important basis for the necessity of groups who define each other as different to maintain a single polity, both in oppositional social movements of civil society or in legislative and other governmental institutions. I have also suggested, however, that the subject of discussion in such a polity should be not restricted to distribution and redistribution of economic resources, or even to issues of control over the means of production and distribution. The way differently identifying groups understand themselves and each other, as well as how their group specific needs and interests intersect with policies and institutions of political decision-making must also be an explicit part of political discourse.

Notes

1 This paper was first presented to the Center for Social Theory and Comparative History at the University of California at Los Angeles in June 1991. Thanks to the participants for a lively discussion. Thanks also to David Alexander and Robert Beauregard for comments on an earlier version. Thanks to Carrie Smarto for research assistance.
2 W.J. Wilson, *The Truly Disadvantaged*, University of Chicago Press, Chicago 1987.
3 See Homi K. Bhabha, 'Interrogating Identity: The Postcolonial Prerogative', in David Goldberg (ed), *Anatomy of Racism*, University of Minnesota Press, Minneapolis 1990.

[4] For more development of how the conception of difference as otherness connects with disgust, see Chapter 5 of my book, *Justice and the Politics of Difference*, Princeton University Press, Princeton 1990.

[5] For an interesting analysis of the structures of enforced heterosexuality and its relation to gender structuring, see Judith Butler, *Gender Troubles*, Routledge, London and New York 1989.

[5] Aysegul Bayakan develops a fascinating account of the identity crisis this process has produced among Turks and those of Turkish descent in Germany. 'The Narrative Construction of the Turkish Immigrant in Germany', unpublished manuscript, Women's Studies, University of Pittsburgh.

[7] Nancy Chodorow developed this idea in her famous paper, 'Family Structure and Feminine Personality', in Rosaldo and Lamphere (eds), *Women, Culture and Society*, Stanford University Press, 1974; see also Nancy Hartsock, *Money, Sex and Power*, Longman, New York 1983.

[8] I have elaborated a description of this process using Julia Kristeva's theory of the abject in Chapter 5 of my book already cited, *Justice and the Politics of Difference*.

[9] For a development of this relational conception of difference, see Martha Minow, *Making All the Difference*, Cornell University Press, Ithaca 1990.

[10] See my 'Impartiality and the Civic Public: Some Implications of Feminist Critiques of Moral and Political Theory', in Cornell and Benhabib (eds), *Feminism as Critique*, U. Minnesota, 1987; and *Justice and the Politics of Difference*, Chapters 4 and 6.

[11] For a well articulated expression of this assimilationist ideal, see Richard Wasserstrom, 'On Racism and Sexism', in *Philosophy and Social Issues*, Notre Dame University Press, Notre Dame 1980.

[12] Michael Sandel, *Liberalism and the Limits of Justice*, Cambridge University Press, Cambridge 1982.

[13] For an extended argument that principles and procedures of 'merit' evaluation cannot be group neutral, see *Justice and the Politics of Difference*, Chapter 7.

[14] This section has benefitted from conversations with Jeff Chekel, Slobodan Pesic, Julie Mostov, and Robert Hayden.

[15] Philip G. Roeder, 'Soviet Federalism and Ethnic Mobilization', *World Politics*, Vol. 43, Jan 1991, pp 196-232.

[16] Jonathan Eyal, 'Eastern Europe: What about the minorities?' *World Today*, Vol 45, December 1989, p 206.

[17] William E. Schmidt, 'Post-Soviet Baltic Republics: Still Stunted and Struggling', *New York Times*, 10 June, 1992.

[18] Robert M. Hayden, 'Constitutional Nationalism in the Formerly Yugoslav Republics', *Slavic Review*, Vol 51, no 4, Fall 1992; see also Julie Mostov, 'Democracy and the Politics of National Identity', paper presented at meetings of the American Political Science Association, Chicaco, August 1992.

[19] See Elez Biber, *Albania: A Socialist Maverick*, Westview Press, Colorado 1990, Chapter 7.

[20] See Veselin Kjuretic, 'The Exodus of the Serbs from Kosovo in the Twentieth Century and Its Political Background', Serbian Academy of Sciences and Arts Institute for Balkan Studies, Belgrade; see also Slobodan M. Pesic, 'Paper on Eastern Europe', Matthew B. Ridgway Center for International Studies, University of Pittsburgh, February 1991.

[21] Andrew Sharp, *Justice and the Maori*, Oxford University Press, Oxford 1990, p 43.

[22] See Augie Fleras, 'Inverting the Bureaucratic Pyramid: Reconciling Aborginality and Bureaucracy in New Zealand', *Journal of the Society for Applied Anthropology*, Vol 48, no 3, Fall 1989, pp 214-225.

Old Themes for New Times Postmodernism, Theory and Cultural Politics

CHRISTOPHER NORRIS

This paper took shape during a period (1991-92) that witnessed, among other melancholy episodes, the return of the British Conservative Government for a fourth consecutive term of office and the outbreak of a large-scale neo-colonialist war fought by the US and its coalition partners in the name of a 'New World Order' equated with Western economic and geo-strategic interests. I abandoned work on the original draft in order to write a book about the Gulf War which tried to explain how large sections of the erstwhile left or left-liberal intelligentsia had been won over to consensus-based doctrines of meaning and truth that left them unable to articulate any kind of reasoned or principled opposition.[1] Critical theory – or what passed itself off as such among postmodernists, post-structuralists, post-Marxists and kindred schools – amounted to a wholesale collapse of moral and intellectual nerve, a line of least resistance that effectively recycled the 'end-of-ideology' rhetoric current in the late 1950s. Francis Fukuyama achieved overnight celebrity on the lecture circuit with his announcement that history had likewise come to an end, since the entire world

– or those parts of it that counted for anything – had converted to capitalism and liberal democracy, thus rendering conflict a thing of the past.[2] Of course there would continue to be trouble-spots, those unfortunate 'Iraqs and Ruritanias' (in Fukuyama's phrase) where the winds of change had yet to penetrate, and where 'crazed dictators' like Saddam Hussein could still create problems for the New World Order.[3] But these regions were beyond the civilized pale, their conflicts 'historical' in the bad old sense, and therefore to be treated – not without regret – as scarcely 'the kind of place that we should wish to make our home'.

The same applied to those internal dissidents and critics of US policy who persisted in raising awkward questions. They might point to the record of Western involvement in the region, the CIA's role in the *coup d'état* that first brought Saddam to power, the various efforts to destabilize his regime when the puppet started pulling (or breaking) the strings, the diplomatic intrigues and economic blackmail that created the alliance of 'Free World' forces lined up against Iraq, the propaganda lies, re-writings of history, manipulated casualty figures, urban mass-destruction covered up by talk of 'precision bombing', 'surgical strikes', 'hi-tech weaponry', the cynical abuses or blatant disregard of UN Security Council resolutions, and other such – albeit contested – matters of record. But these critics merely signalled their own chronic failure to catch up with the current rules of the game, the fact that we had now, at last, moved on into a 'post-ideological' epoch where consensus values and beliefs held sway, and where nothing could count as valid grounds for dissent among those bred on a decent respect for liberal democracy, market capitalism and the emergent New World Order. To suppose otherwise – to treat all this as just a cultural propaganda-line in the service of US hegemonic interests – was merely a sign of one's still being hooked on old-style (Marxist or Enlightenment) notions like truth, ideology or critique. Quite simply there was now *no difference* between what the majority could be brought to think and what was true for all practical purposes. The 'end of history' was also an end to those deluded self-aggrandizing notions on the part of critical intellectuals who had once defined their role in principled opposition to the ideological self-images of the age. Such ideas could no longer have any place in a liberal consensus – or postmodern polity – happily delivered from the conflicts thus induced by questioning one's fortunate role as a citizen in this best of all possible worlds.

In *Uncritical Theory* I described this picture as one whose 'sublime naivety and lack of historical perspective could only have exerted such widespread appeal at a time when many people (intellectuals and political analysts among them) were eager to substitute the reassuring placebos of consensus belief for the effort to criticize US policy in light of its real-world consequences and effects.'[4] And I argued that the same diagnosis should apply to postmodernism, neopragmatism, post-structuralism and kindred movements which were busily engaged in reducing all truth-claims to a species of rhetorical imposition, assimilating history to the realm of narrative contrivance, and rubbishing 'Enlightenment' values and beliefs in whatever residual form. Thus commentators in journals like *Marxism Today* (whose very title had by then become something of a standing joke) queued up to renounce any lingering attachment to such old-hat notions as truth, reason, critique, ideology, or false consciousness. Whatever their doubts with regard to Fukuyama and his 'end-of-history' thesis, at least they were united in rejecting · those ideas as having now been overtaken by the passage to a postmodern ('New Times') outlook that acknowledged the collapse of any hopes once vested in Marxism or other such delusory 'meta-narrative' creeds.[5] This realignment of theoretical positions on the Left went along with a widespread tactical retreat from socialist principles among Labour Party politicians, policy-makers, media and academic pundits. Such thinking was presented as a victory for the 'new realism', for a programme that sensibly adjusted its sights to the horizon of a broad-based popular appeal defined in accordance with the latest opinion-poll feedback. On a range of issues (nuclear

disarmament, trade union law, privatization, public sector
funding) it was thought to be in Labour's best electoral
interests to adopt a more pragmatic line.

For on one point at least the commentators were agreed:
that elections were no longer won or lost on the strength of
valid arguments, appeals to moral justice, or even to
enlightened self-interest on the part of a reasonably
well-informed electorate. What counted now was the
ability to seize the high ground of public opinion
management by adopting strategies that faithfully
mirrored the perceived self-image of the times. No matter
if this led to a series of policy climb-downs that inevitably
left the Labour leadership exposed to charges of
inconstancy or downright cynical opportunism. No matter
if it rested on a *false* consensus. For to raise such objections
was merely to demonstrate one's failure to move with the
times, or one's attachment to hopelessly outworn ideas of
truth, right reason, or ethical accountability.

Of course there would always be socialist diehards who
continued to think that way, to believe that a sizeable
proportion of the electorate had nothing to gain – and a
lot to lose – from a further period of Conservative rule.
But these figures were marginalized to the point of
near-invisibility by a kind of tacit cross-party alliance which
locked the whole 'debate' into a meaningless charade, a
pseudo-contest where the main concern was how best to
massage the various illusions and forms of false
consciousness that effectively decided the outcome. Such
techniques had long been the stock-in-trade of Conservative propaganda, depending on an appeal to the lowest
common denominators of ignorance, prejudice and
entrenched self-interest. The only thing different about
this campaign was the extent to which Labour went along
with the charade. Thus there was little to choose between
the parties save a Tory rhetoric of 'incentives', 'self-help',
'free enterprise' and 'market forces' *versus* a Labour
rhetoric that likewise took those values on board, but
which shied away from their harsher implications through
the adoption of various qualifying adjuncts (such as the
'social market').

Small wonder that the end of all this pragmatist adjustment was a situation where many perplexed voters opted for the dubious comfort of sticking with the devils they knew. And on the intellectual left the same orthodox wisdom prevailed. Thus it was taken as read that Labour's only chance was to update its image by adopting a rhetoric more consonant with these new (postmodern, post-industrial or 'post-Fordist') times.[6] In the process it would need to dump old alliances, among them its close relationship with the unions, its traditional reliance on a strong base of working-class support, and its claims to represent or articulate such interests in the name of a better, more just and egalitarian social order. These principles no longer held much appeal – it was argued – for an increasingly *déclassé* electorate whose allegiances had more to do with social aspiration – with Conservative talk of 'upward mobility' and a 'classless society' – than with facts like unemployment, urban deprivation, the run-down of public services, or the emergence of a two-tier system in health care and education. To harp on about the Tory record in office was a mistake, the pundits urged, since it ignored the extent to which voters could identify with an upbeat rhetoric (however remote from their present situation and real future prospects) which clearly struck a responsive chord among many of Labour's erstwhile or potential supporters. Only by abandoning the moral high ground could the Party hope to win back the confidence of voters in its crucial target groups.

What this advice came down to was a domesticated version of the wider postmodernist outlook, that is to say, a line of argument that renounced all notions of truth, principle or genuine (as opposed to imaginary) interests, and which counselled that those values henceforth be replaced with a straightforward appeal to whatever seemed best in the way of short-term electoral advantage. More specifically, it involved four major premises: first, that for all practical purposes truth is synonymous with consensus belief; second, that ideology (or 'false conscious-ness') is an outmoded concept along with other such Marxist/Enlightenment doctrines; third, that any talk of 'class' or 'class interests' was likewise a chronic liability, given the changed (and immensely more complex) conditions of present-day social experience; and fourth that these conditions required a complete rethinking of Labour's claims to 'represent' any actual or emergent community of interests. What might be left of 'socialism' at the end of this revisionist road was a question that the pundits preferred not to raise, unless by according it – as many now advised – the dignity of a decent burial.

When the results came through one might have expected some modification of this line, or at least some acknowledgement that pragmatism had not paid off, and that perhaps it was time for a long hard look at matters of policy and principle. On the contrary, the first postmortem articles were off on exactly the same tack, arguing (as in a *New Statesman & Society* piece by Stuart Hall) that Labour had betrayed its own best interests by *not going far enough* along the revisionist path.[7] The litmus-test here was the issue of tax reform and redistribution of wealth, since it offered the sole instance of an election pledge where Labour had – albeit very cautiously – ventured to challenge the consensus wisdom. Although there was heartening evidence that this policy enjoyed support even among voters in the projected high-tax band who agreed ('in principle') that the extra burden would be more than offset by wider social benefits, in the event it appears either that many people switched votes at the eleventh hour, or that they had intended to vote Conservative all along, but concealed the fact as simply too shameful to acknowledge. The post-election consensus was that this had been yet another great mistake on Labour's part, a piece of high-minded policy-making which once again revealed the widening gap between socialist principle and the 'realities' of life as currently perceived by voters in the electorally crucial interest-groups. As Stuart Hall put it:

> the shadow budget's tax bands gave Labour the look of punitive vindictiveness. It drew the line where, realistically,

it reckoned people could afford it, forgetting that in post-Thatcher Britain, people calculate their tax liabilities not on what they actually earn, but how much they hope, desire or aspire to earn in the very near future. Labour was playing the economics of realism and fiscal rectitude. The Tories played the 'sociology of aspirations'.[8]

The language of this passage would repay close analysis in the style of Raymond Williams' *Keywords*; that is to say, a socio-cultural anatomy of the times based on the semantic structures implicit in certain ideologically loaded terms.[9] To be 'realist' in such matters, on this account, was to abandon that other, more pragmatic or efficacious kind of 'realism' which might have carried Labour to victory had its strategists only taken heed of the opinion polls and not indulged their old, vote-losing fondness for values like truth, reason and principle. Such values count for little, so the argument runs, as compared with those 'hopes and aspirations' which the Conservatives were much better able to exploit by appealing to a highly seductive realm of imaginary wish-fulfilment.

Stuart Hall would most likely reject any comparison between this kind of hard-headed 'realist' assessment and Baudrillard's wholesale postmodernist espousal of a 'hyperreality' that negates all distinctions between truth and falsehood, fact and fiction, real human needs and their simulated counterparts as purveyed by the opinion polls and market-research agencies.[10] His essay is after all a serious contribution to debate, written from a standpoint of sober diagnostic hindsight, and hence worlds apart from Baudrillard's style of puckish nihilist abandon. But this does seem to be the direction in which his arguments are headed, especially in view of the way that 'realism' shifts over, in the course of his article, from a usage that signifies something like 'old-fashioned socialist respect for the truth-telling virtues' to a sense much more within the Baudrillard range, the 'willingness to play the postmodern game and make the most of one's chances through a "realist" appeal to the current self-images of the age'. It is hard to know how else one should interpret passages like the following:

Bland and colourless as he is, Mr Major may indeed be
finely tuned, as a political symbol, to these intricate (and
perhaps self-deceiving) attempts to square the circle, and
to the other underlying sociological and aspirational shifts
in the electorate that have taken place. His meritocratic
'decency' registers with extraordinary precision exactly
that balance between the desire for a more 'caring'
self-image, which led committed Thatcherites, with heavy
hearts, to ditch Mrs Thatcher, and that deeply self-
interested calculation, which remains her enduring
contribution.[11]

On the one hand, this acknowledges the specious
character of John Major's electoral appeal, his continuation of Thatcherite policies under a different (more
'caring' and 'decent') rhetorical guise, and the extent to
which voters had been taken in by this superficial switch of
style. On the other, it veers away from any such realist
judgment, 'realist' in the strong sense of maintaining the
distinction between truth and falsehood, or allowing that
those electors were actually *wrong* – deceived by the
rhetoric of their own 'aspirational' self-image into voting
as they did. What Hall cannot countenance is any hint of a
return to notions like 'ideology' or 'false consciousness',
terms that might provide the beginning of an answer to
the questions posed by his article.

Thus Hall's talk of 'squaring the circle' applies most
aptly to his own attempt to explain this phenomenon while
denying himself recourse to the only adequate explanatory concepts. On a postmodernist reading of the signs
there is simply no escaping the closed circuit – the
pseudo-logic of specular misrecognition – which accounts
for John Major as a 'finely tuned' (albeit a 'bland and
colourless') symbol of voter aspirations, while viewing the
electorate as a passive reflector of those same imaginary
interests. 'Imaginary', that is, for the majority of voters
who would surely lose out (on any realist reckoning) once
the Tories were returned to power. Of course there were
others whose 'real' (if selfish and short-term) interests
John Major could plausibly claim to represent, and who
thus had cause (if not justification) for welcoming the

outcome. But Hall is in no position to remark such differences, resting as they do on a prior set of distinctions – real/imaginary, true/false, knowledge/ideology – which he regards as simply obsolescent. Not that he wishes to dump the whole baggage of socialist aims and principles. Indeed he goes so far as to acknowledge that these are still 'decent' values, that Labour fought a 'decent' campaign, and that even its fiscal policy was justified by the existing maldistribution of wealth. Nor is the reader left in any doubt as to Hall's grim prognosis for the coming electoral term. Thus:

> under his [Major's] benign regime, Thatcherism as a model of social transformation will continue to work its way through the system. By the time we are allowed to vote again, education, public transport and the welfare state will have been reconstructed along the two-track lines of the National Health Service, and broadcasting will have succumbed to the new brutalism. Everything in life will be 'private' ('I have, of course, no intention of privatising the NHS') – in the sense of privately owned, run, or managed, driven by the short-term model or powered by the self-interested, profit-motivated goals of British bosses, the most philistine and least successful ruling class in the Western world. In this sense, Mr Major is child and heir of Thatcherism, smile and smile as he may.[12]

One could hardly wish for a clearer, more forthright and impassioned statement of the social evils likely to follow from another four years of Conservative rule. Certainly Stuart Hall has no desire to line up with the chorus of ideologues, tabloid commentators, business analysts and captains of industry in greeting the election result as yet another chance to proclaim the demise of socialism. But they could well take comfort from his other, more 'realist' line of argument concerning the need for Labour to move with the times and adapt its image to the currency of consensus belief. In the end this amounts to a vote of 'no confidence' in any kind of reasoned or principled socialist case that would counter the drift toward a politics based entirely on the workings of (real or illusory) self-interest.

It seems to me that the lessons to be learned from Labour's defeat were precisely the opposite of those proferred by Stuart Hall and other commentators of a 'New Times'/postmodernist persuasion. The first lesson concerns the inbuilt limits of a pragmatist approach that goes all out for electoral appeal by abandoning even the most basic standards of reason, consistency, and truth. In this sense there was justice in the charge against Labour that its about-turn on the issue of nuclear disarmament was merely a tactical ploy, having nothing to do with any change of conviction or realist assessment of the altered geopolitical state of affairs. By taking the line of least resistance Labour relinquished not only the moral high ground but its chance to argue a case much strengthened by this turn in real-world events.

Let me quote one further passage from Hall's article which exemplifies some of the moral and intellectual contortions produced by this effort to analyse Labour's defeat from a post-ideological standpoint.

> Choice, opportunity to rise, mobility within one's lifetime, the power to decide your own fate, where anyone, whatever his or her background, can becoming anything, provided they work hard enough; this is what Mr Major means by 'classlessness' and 'a society at ease with itself'. The claim appears ludicrous to more egalitarian folk. But it is exactly the kind of 'accessible classlessness' that millions believe to be desirable and realistic, and exactly the kind of low-powered motor that takes Majorism beyond traditional Tory areas into a new arena where new constituencies are there to be won. This is the voice that was heard in Basildon and a thousand new 'classless' working-class and surburban communities across the country, the heartland of the new 'sociology of aspirations'.[13]

Stuart Hall knows full well how bogus was this appeal to a 'classless' society that existed only as a figment of the social imaginary, projected on the one hand by shrewd Tory strategists with an eye to the electoral main chance, and on the other by those 'millions' who doubtless believed such a prospect to be both 'desirable' and 'realistic'. He also knows that there is a difference between wish and reality;

that voter 'aspirations' were expertly played upon in the course of the election campaign; and that they bore no resemblance – outside this imaginary realm – to anything that might with reason be expected from a further five years of Conservative rule. Hall knows all this at the level of straightforward knowledge-by-acquaintance, but when it comes to drawing the relevant lessons there are things that Hall either chooses to ignore or somehow cannot bring himself to 'know'. Among them are three salient points: that many people voted against their own and the country's best interests; that they did so for ideological reasons; and that despite being out of fashion as a concept among present-day critical theorists 'false consciousness' still has some useful explanatory work to do.

Hall's reluctance to concede these facts gives rise to some curious argumentative and rhetorical shifts. The symptoms appear in those queasy quotation-marks around phrases like 'accessible classlessness', 'sociology of aspirations', and 'a society at ease with itself'. For the passage simply won't disclose whether we should take them at face value (i.e., as both 'desirable' and 'realistic') or whether, on the contrary, they are best treated from a critical, diagnostic, or socio-pathological standpoint. To opt for the first reading would amount to a line of unresisting acquiescence in whatever the opinion-polls happened to say, or whatever people could be brought to accept through forms of manufactured consensus belief. It would thus mark the end of any socialist hopes for a better, more just or humane social order achieved by criticizing false beliefs and exposing their imaginary (ideological) character. But from a 'New Times' perspective this looks too much like the old Marxist or Enlightenment line, the arrogant idea that intellectuals are somehow entitled to speak up for truth, reason or principle as against the current self-images of the age. Thus Hall works round to the odd position of recognizing 'Majorism' for the hollow fraud that it is – a re-run of Marx's *Eighteenth Brumaire*, with Thatcher and Major standing in for Napoleon and *Napoléon le petit* – while denying himself the conceptual and ethical resources to come straight out and acknowledge the fact. And this despite his often clear-eyed perception of the means by which voters were persuaded to endorse a mystified version of their own real interests as purveyed by the Tory media.

One could make the same point about Hall's remark that such popular hopes and aspirations must appear ludicrous 'to more egalitarian folk'. For this prompts the obvious questions: does Hall still count himself among their number, or has he now moved on with these postmodern times to the stage of abandoning all such high-toned talk? *Either* Hall believes (as surely he does) that egalitarian and socialist principles are still worth upholding, *or* (to judge solely by the passage in hand) he has redefined 'socialism' in such a way as to sever its links with any principled commitment to notions of equality, social justice, or redistribution of wealth. This is the real irony of Hall's analysis: that in leaning so far towards consensus-values (or refusing to endorse a critique of those values in ideological terms) he effectively denies any prospect of escaping from the goldfish-bowl of imaginary misrecognition. Then there is the reference to Basildon, a place-name that will surely be fixed in the memory of anyone who stayed up late on election night to see the results come in. For Basildon was a Conservative-held seat high on the list of Labour's looked-for gains if it was to stand much chance of forming the next government. What made this result even more crucial as an index of the way things were going was the fact that Basildon presented such a challenge to conventional demographic methods for predicting electoral trends. Situated in the border-zone between London and Essex, home to a great many upwardly mobile voters, and representing, as Hall rightly notes, the very heartland of the 'new sociology of aspirations', Basildon was a feather in the wind for psephologists and other watchers of the pre-election scene. In the event it was among the first results to be declared and marked the turn from predictions of a workable Labour majority to acknowledgement that the Conservatives were back in power.

So Stuart Hall has good reason for his choice of Basildon as a test-case in light of the election result. But there is a crucial difference between analyzing the causes which conspired to produce that result, and holding it out as a model instance of the kinds of voter-appeal that Labour would have done well to cultivate. In this case pragmatism (in its 'Majorite' form) would define the agenda of political debate not only for the Basildon electorate but also for those others who sought to learn the lessons of electorate defeat and adapt more successfully the next time around. After all, John Major 'embodies the growing number of people who, though not mystified about their humble class origins, no longer believe they should remain, as he puts it, "boxed in" to them forever'. Moreover, according to Hall, 'he articulates this attitude, not in terms of the reality of, but the *aspiration to*, social mobility, and the ethic of personal achievement'. What can it mean to be non-mystified about issues of class and social origin if this promotes a mind-set perfectly attuned to John Major's spurious *déclassé* rhetoric, or a groundswell of imaginary identification with class-interests so remote from those of even the most upwardly-mobile Basildon voter? How should we interpret such talk of an 'ethic of personal fulfilment' if not by realistically translating it back into the language of straightforward Thatcherite greed, self-interest or acquisitive individualism? What remains of the socialist argument against these values if one adopts a new 'realism' (or a 'new sociology of aspirations') which models itself so closely on the style and techniques of Tory campaign management? And why assume that Basildon points the only way forward for a re-think of Labour strategy in light of its latest electoral defeat?

One might have thought, on the contrary, that any lessons to be learned from 'Basildon 1992' had to do not so much with Labour's need to back down on yet more of its socialist principles as with its need to stand by those principles, communicate them more effectively, and combat their malicious and distorted presentation in the organs of Tory propaganda. It would indeed be cause for despair if the 'voice of Basildon' were taken as a truly representative sample, an instance of those 'heartland' communities that Labour has to win by ditching its every

last policy commitment and espousing a rhetoric of
' "classless" working-class' values. This message may
perhaps carry credence with cultural critics of a
post-Marxist 'New Times' persuasion, otherwise there
would seem little merit in resting one's case for policy
review very largely on the vagaries of a localized
melting-pot constituency where voting behaviour can
better be analyzed in causal-symptomatic than in rational
terms. Stuart Hall of course draws the opposite
conclusion, lamenting Labour's failure to press far enough
with its revisionist line: 'the adaptation has been too
shallow, painful without cutting deep ... More the kind of
face-lift marketing men give an old product when
launching it with a new package, less a shift of political
culture and strategy rooted in the configurations of
modern social change.' In effect this attempts to turn the
tables on all those old-fashioned, high-toned moralists by
suggesting that the *principled* course would have been for
Labour to conduct such a wholesale policy review, as
contrasted with a shifty compromise approach or wary
revisionism that lacked the courage of its own pragmatist
convictions. Nothing could be further from the truth;
what the election results bore home with painful clarity –
and nowhere more so than in Basildon – was the fact that
Labour could only lose out by playing the Tories at their
own cynical game.

   On Stuart Hall's account the best electoral strategy
would have been one that pushed right through with this
revisionist programme, implicit in his call for a
thoroughgoing 'shift of political culture and strategy'
responsive to the 'configurations of modern social change'.
In fact Hall's phrase is 'rooted in', which suggests
something more like a Gramscian organic relation, a
quasi-naturalized elective affinity between socio-economic
structures and their articulation at the level of cultural
values and political beliefs. But there is no room here for
the role that Gramsci attributes to 'critical' intellectuals,
those thinkers who challenge the dominant ideology from
a dissident standpoint identified with interests that are
marginalzied by the current consensus.[14] For they could

exercise this role only in so far as such interests achieved articulate expression *over and against* the prevailing set of values, beliefs, or cultural self-images. And this would in turn require a stronger (more adequately theorized) account of 'ideology' than anything allowed for by Hall's consensualist model, that is, his understanding of 'political culture and strategy' as a matter of finely tuned feedback response, or rapid adjustment to the latest opinion-poll findings. What drops out of sight on this analysis is the difference between real and imaginary interests, or the extent to which people can be swung into accepting a false – systematically distorted – view of those interests through various well-tried suasive techniques.

Clearly there would be small hope of success for any future socialist strategy which completely ignored the demographic shifts, the new 'sociology of aspirations' noted by observers like Hall. Such data provide the indispensable starting-point for a politics aware of the problems it confronts in overcoming those forms of imaginary investment (or ideological misrecognition) so effectively exploited by Conservative Central Office and its allies in the tabloid press. But this is not to say that the only realistic way forward for Labour is to tailor its appeal to the image given back by those same (however accurate or in some sense representative) findings. For it is a counsel of despair, a no-win policy even in tactical terms, to adopt this pragmatist line of least resistance and thus offer nothing but a softened-up version of Tory electoral strategy. Given such a choice many voters will feel that they might as well opt for the genuine article – for a politics frankly wedded to the values of self-interest and appetitive individualism – rather than one that concedes those values in a shamefaced or opportunist manner.

Of course there is the danger of arrogance, complacency or worse in the use of terms like 'ideology' and 'false consciousness', terms that may connote an offensively us-and-them attitude, a presumption of superior (undeluded) knowledge on the part of enlightened leftist intellectuals. In Terry Eagleton's words, 'I view things as they really are; you squint at them through a tunnel vision imposed by some extraneous system of doctrine.' Or again: 'His thought is red-neck, yours is doctrinal, and mine is deliciously supple.'[15] After all, as Eagleton bluntly remarks, 'nobody would claim that their own thinking was ideological, just as nobody would habitually refer to themselves as Fatso ... Ideology, like halitosis, is in this sense what the other person has.'[16] No doubt the desire not to strike such an attitude plays its part in current variations on the pragmatist, postmodernist or end-of-ideology theme. It is likewise a factor in commentaries on the British polical scene which understandably back off from imputing 'false consciousness' to a sizeable portion of the electorate, or from setting themselves up as somehow in possession of a truth denied to those other, more benighted types. But one should also bear in mind Stuart Hall's reference to the illusions suffered by those well-meaning 'egalitarian folk' who continued to believe, despite all the signs, that socialism cannot or should not make terms with the reality of social injustice. For it is they (Hall implies) who must nowadays be seen as the real dupes of ideology, that is to say, of an attitude which vainly persists in distinguishing truth from its various 'imaginary' or 'ideological' surrogates. What thus starts out as a decent respect for the other person's viewpoint, or a dislike of high-handed moralizing talk, in the end becomes a kind of reverse discrimination, a refusal to conceive that anyone could have grounds (reasoned and principled grounds) for adopting such a dissident stance. And this would apply not only to left intellectuals hooked on notions like truth, critique, or ideology but also to those credulous old-guard types – among them the majority of Labour voters – who persist in the sadly deluded belief that 'socialism' means something other and more than a shuffling adjustment to the signs of the times.

The debates around postmodernism in philosophy, criticism and cultural theory may appear far removed from the doldrums of present-day British and US politics. All the same I think it is worth pursuing the connection –

at very least, the elective affinity – between this *au courant* talk of 'New Times' on the post-Marxist left and that strain of ultra-nominalist sceptical thought for which the sublime figures as a limit-point of language or representation, a point where (according to theorists like Lyotard) philosophy comes up against a salutary check to its truth-telling powers and prerogatives. These are specialized concerns, sure enough, and unlikely to rank very high on the list of anyone seeking a persuasive diagnosis of contemporary social and political ills. But the connection may appear less remote if one considers some of Lyotard's claims with regard to the Kantian sublime, a topos whose extraordinary prestige and prominence in recent critical debate can hardly be explained without taking stock of that wider cultural context.[17] For what the sublime gives us to reflect upon, in Lyotard's account, is the absolute 'heterogeneity' of phrase-regimes, the gulf (or 'differend') that exists between judgments in the cognitive or epistemic mode and judgments of an ethical, political, or evaluative nature.[18] These latter cannot (should not) be subjected to the same kinds of validity-condition that standardly apply with phrases in the domain of factual or historical knowledge. That is to say, they belong to a realm quite apart from that of theoretical understanding, where the rule is that phenomenal intuitions must be 'brought under' concepts by way of ascertaining its operative powers and limits. For there is always the danger (so Kant warns us) that philosophy will overstep those limits, pursuing all manner of metaphysical ideas which may be perfectly legitimate in themselves – bearing on the interests of reason in its pure or speculative modes – but which can have no basis in our knowledge of the world as given by the forms of sensuous cognition and adequate conceptual grasp.[19]

To confuse these realms is a mistake which leads to some large and damaging consequences. On the one hand, it exposes theoretical enquiry (science and the cognitive disciplines) to a range of bewildering distractions, projects that begin by aiming beyond their epistemological reach, and which frequently end up by reactively adopting some posture of extravagant sceptical doubt. On the other hand, it tends to annul the distinction – so vital for Kantian ethics – between *determinate* judgments (having to do with matters of causal consequence, factual truth or logical necessity) and *reflective* judgments that issue from the sphere of 'suprasensible' ideas or principles, and which thus secure a space for the exercise of freely willed autonomous agency and choice. Any confusions here are apt to produce the worst of both worlds, an illusory freedom or unrestrained speculative licence in the realm of theoretical understanding and a bleakly reductive, determinist outlook with regard to ethical issues. Hence the significance of the Kantian sublime as a name for that which somehow 'presents the unpresentable', or which calls forth an order of affective response beyond what is given us to think or understand at the level of cognitive judgment. Hence also its attraction for Lyotard and other revisionist readers of Kant, anxious as they are to play down his attachment to the philosophic discourse of modernity and to stress those aspects of his thinking which supposedly prefigure our current 'postmodern condition'. But the result of such readings is a perverse misconstrual of the Kantian project which elevates the sublime to absolute pride of place, and which does so solely in pursuit of its own irrationalist or counter-Enlightenment aims.

This emerges most clearly in Lyotard's extreme version of the incommensurability thesis, his idea that there exists a multiplicity of language-games (or 'phrase-regimes') each with its own *sui generis* criteria of meaning, validity or truth. From which it follows – again by analogy with the Kantian sublime, or Lyotard's reading thereof – that the cognitive phrase-regime not only has to yield up its privileged truth-telling role, but must also be seen as committing a form of speech-act injustice (a suppression of the narrative 'differend') whenever it presumes to arbitrate in matters of ethical or political justice. What this amounts to, in short, is a postmodern variant on the drastic dichotomy between fact and value standardly (though wrongly) attributed to Hume, allied to a strain of out-and-out nominalism which denies that statements can have any meaning – any truth-

value, purport or operative force – aside from the manifold
language-games that make up an ongoing cultural conversation. Only by seeking to maximize narrative differentials, by cultivating 'dissensus' or 'heterogeneity', can thinking be sure to remain on guard against those kinds of coercive (and potentially totalitarian) phrase-regimes that have so far exerted their malign hold upon the discourse of 'enlightened' reason.

It is wrong, so Lyotard would argue, to adduce historical or factual considerations, when assessing the significance of 'great events' like the French Revolution, the Nazi death-camps, or other charged and evocative phrases whose meaning eludes such criteria. For this is to confuse the two distinct orders of truth-claim, on the one hand, those that properly have to do with issues of empirical warrant, eye-witness testimony, archival research etc.; and on the other hand, those that can only find expression in a language whose evaluative character precludes any straightforward appeal to the facts of the case. The crucial point here is the way that certain *names* are taken up into a range of contending discourses which then set the terms, or establish their own criteria, for what should count as a truthful, relevant, or good-faith assertion. Those names would be 'rigid designators' (in Kripke's parlance) only to the extent that they served to pick out persons, places or dates whose reference, in some minimal sense of the word, could be taken pretty much for granted.[20] Beyond that they would evoke such deep-laid disagreement that the names would function more as surrogate descriptors, nominal points of intersection for a variety of language-games, narrative paradigms, imputed attributes, ethical judgments etc., each of them assigning its own significance to the term in question. Such names might include (to mix some of Lyotard's examples with some of my own) 'Napoleon', 'Marx', 'Lenin', 'Hitler', 'Auschwitz', 'Leningrad', 'Dunkirk', 'October 1917', 'Berlin 1953', 'Prague 1968', 'Berlin 1990', 'Baghdad 1991', and others of a kindred character.[21] In every case, according to Lyotard, their utterance gives rise to a strictly irreducible conflict of interpretations, a dispute (or differend) between rival claims as to their 'true' historical meaning.

Least of all can such issues be resolved through an attempt to establish what actually occurred, or to offer more adequate (factual or evidential) grounds for arriving at a properly informed estimate. For on Lyotard's account there is simply no passage – no possible means of translation – from the phrase-regime of cognitive (or factual-documentary) truth to the phrase-regimes of ethics, political justice, or other evaluative speech-act genres. And this rule must apply, he maintains, even when confronted with apparently outrageous instances, like Faurisson's right-wing 'revisionist' claim that for all we can know the gas-chambers never existed, since there survive no witnesses who can vouch for the fact on the basis of first-hand experience or knowledge-by-acquaintance. Of course it may be said that such arguments amount to nothing more than a vicious sophistry, an effort to obscure or deny the truth by adopting criteria grossly inappropriate to the case in hand. But this is to miss the point, according to Lyotard, since Faurisson has not the slightest interest in getting things right by the normative standards of responsible (truth-seeking) scholarly enquiry. Nor, for that matter, is Faurisson much concerned with issues of right and wrong as conceived by most historians of the Holocaust, those for whom the interests of factual truth are indissociable from questions of moral accountability or good-faith ethical judgment. On the contrary: 'the historian need not strive to convince Faurisson if Faurisson is "playing" another genre of discourse, one in which conviction, or the attainment of consensus over a defined reality, is not at stake.'[22] Opponents may have good reason – at least by their own disciplinary or moral lights – for denouncing Faurisson as a rabid ideologue, a sophistical perverter of the truth, or a pseudo-historian whose 'revisionist' project is a cover for the crudest kind of anti-Semitic propaganda. But they will be wrong so to argue, Lyotard thinks. For quite simply there is *no common ground* between Faurisson and those who reject his views, whether professional historians affronted by his cavalier way with the documentary evidence or non-specialists appalled by his indifference to the manifest evils of Nazism and the suffering of its victims.

To suppose otherise is a temptation that Faurisson's critics would do well to resist. Such rejoinders will in any case be wholly ineffective, failing as they do to acknowledge the differend – the radical heterogeneity – that separates his discourse from theirs. But they will also run the risk of his turning the tables, accusing his accusers of practising a language-game (referential, cognitive, factual-documentary or whatever) that not only ignores but actively suppresses the crucial point at issue between them. In Lyotard's words, '[i]f the demand to have to establish the reality of the referent of a sentence is extended to any sentence ... then that demand is totalitarian in its principle.'[23] So it is better to accept that there is nothing to be gained by disputing Faurisson's 'arguments' as if these were subject to the normal criteria or validity-conditions for statements of historical truth. Given such a downright clash of heterogeneous discourse – of beliefs, values, ideologies, phrase-regimes, or narrative paradigms – the best that one can do is renounce any prospect of engaging in reasoned argumentative debate. Thus 'Auschwitz' must figure as one of those names whose significance cannot be established by any amount of patient archival research, since it so far exceeds our powers of understanding, of adequate conceptual grasp, as to render such debate otiose.

This is where the sublime comes in, once again, as an index of the gulf between factual truth-claims and judgments of an evaluative or ethico-political order. For what the death-camps signify (according to Lyotard) is an event beyond all the capacities of rational thought, an event that stands as the ultimate rebuke to 'Enlightenment' aims and principles. At this point, he writes,

> something new has happened in history (which can only be a sign and not a fact) which is that the facts, the testimonies, which bore the traces of *heres* and *nows*, the documents which indicated the meaning or meanings of the facts, and the names, finally the possibility of diverse kinds of phrases whose conjunction makes reality, all this has been destroyed as much as possible.[24]

If 'reality' (or historical truth) were indeed just a matter of 'phrases' – a construct out of various descriptions, vocabularies, language-games, tropes, and narratives – then one might (just about) make tolerable sense of Lyotard's argument. And of course such ideas are pretty much *de rigueur* among the adepts of postmodern and post-structuralist theory, those for whom the referent is a fictive postulate, a redundant third term whose role has been eclipsed (since Saussure) by our knowledge of the 'arbitrary' relation between signifier and signified. Otherwise the passage will serve as a cautionary reminder of the sceptical extremes to which 'theory' may be driven when divorced from any sense of real-world cognitive and moral accountability. For it is a *fact* (not an 'idea' in Lyotard's quasi-Kantian usage of the term) that Auschwitz existed, that it became one of the sites for the Nazi programme of mass-extermination, that the gas-chambers functioned as a part of that programme, and moreover – as will surely be agreed by any but the most blinkered of 'revisionist' ideologues – that there exists an overwhelming mass of evidence to prove that this was the case. Nor would Faurisson's lies (or Lyotard's scepticism) be in any way justified even if it were true that 'all this' (the documentary evidence) had in fact been 'destroyed as much as possible'. For witness to the event would still be borne by those material traces that were not (or could not be) so destroyed, together with the archives, the depositions of death-camp survivors, and the testimony of convicted war-crime defendants.

Of course the sceptic may then wish to argue that such evidence is 'textual' in the sense of being open to various interpretations, one of which (namely, Faurisson's) will reject it out of hand, while another (Lyotard's) will defend a form of principled agnosticism, a refusal to privilege any reading which seeks to have the last word.[25] And indeed there is no refuting this position, unless by various forms of *reductio ad absurdum* argument, whereby the sceptic is shown to inhabit a solipsistic world (or textualist prison-house) of his or her own devizing. For they can still refuse to play by the commonsense, rational, good-faith or realist rules, declaring such rules to be simply irrelevant –

no part of their chosen language-game – and preferring to stick with their position whatever its consequences. But it is important to be clear about those consequences, especially in view of Lyotard's claim that we can only do justice to the rival litigants in any given case by respecting the speech-art or narrative differend between them, and thus suspending all judgments of truth and falsehood or right and wrong. What this 'justice' means with regard to Faurisson is that the sceptic *has every right* to assert that the gas-chambers never existed, or were never put to the purpose of mass-extermination, just so long as he allows others the right to maintain a contrary opinion according to their own cognitive and ethical criteria.

Thus they might well respond by remarking – like Stephen Greenblatt in a recent essay – that the Nazis, so far from destroying all the evidence, in fact displayed an equal and opposite compulsion to amass huge amounts of it, including those collections of personal effects, bodily remains, hair, teeth-fillings and other such grim testimonials to the nature and scale of their atrocities.[26] Nor (presumably) would Lyotard deny the evidential force of such arguments or their claim upon the conscience of anyone committed to establishing the truth of what happened. All the same, 'positivist historians are at the mercy of a Faurisson if they imagine that justice consists solely in the application of cognitive rules in such cases.' And again, '[i]f history were merely a question of such rules, it is hard to know how Faurisson could be accused of injustice.'[27] For it is only through the exercise of interpretive freedom (a freedom unconstrained by cognitivist appeals to the known, reconstructed, or empirically warranted facts of the case) that opponents can claim any ethical right to criticize Faurisson's arguments. And even then they will be subject to the charge of suppressing the differend or imposing their own criteria for debate if they seek to discredit Faurisson by appeal to truth-claims or ethical values that he simply won't acknowledge. In such cases,

> one side's legitimacy does not imply the other's lack of legitimacy. Applying a single rule of judgment to both in

order to settle their differend ... would wrong (at least) one
of them (and both of them if neither side accepts this rule)
... A wrong results from the fact that the rules of the genre
of discourse by which one judges are not those of the
judged genre or genres of discourse.[28]

This passage shows just how far Lyotard is willing to travel
along the path to an ultra-nominalist position where
language-games (or speech-act genres) go all the way
down, and where issues of truth are wholly subsumed to
issues of linguistic (or textual) representation. Like so
much postmodern and post-structuralist theory, it begins
by setting up a straw-man opponent – the unreconstructed
'positivist' – and ends by renouncing any claim to
adjudicate in questions of truth and right. That he is
willing to apply such arguments to an instance like
Auschwitz, and (in effect) accord Faurisson the benefit of
the sceptical doubt, is a sign of the moral confusions
brought about by this most extreme variant of the
present-day 'linguistic turn'.

The same confusions are visible (albeit in less spectacular
form) when Lyotard addresses political issues of class,
ideology, and representation. Here again he falls back on
the sublime as a kind of postmodernist shibboleth, a reminder – as if any were needed – of the problems confronted by
left intellectuals who still seek to make sense of history from
a standpoint of class-based *Ideologiekritik*. His response to
Terry Eagleton during a 1985 debate at the Institute of
Contemporary Arts in London is a fair enough sample of
Lyotard's reflections in this quasi-Kantian vein.

Nobody has ever seen a proletariat (Marx said this): you
can observe working classes, certainly, but they are only
part of the observable society. It's impossible to argue that
this part of society is the incarnation of the proletariat,
because an Idea in general has no presentation, and *that is
the question of the sublime* ... I'm sure we have to read and
re-read Marx, but in a critical way: that is, we must say that
the question of the proletariat is the question of knowing
whether this word is to be understood in terms of the
Hegelian dialectic (that is to say, in the end, in terms of
science), expecting to find something experiential to

correspond to the concept, and maybe to the concept itself;
or is the term 'proletariat' the name of an Idea of Reason,
the name of a subject to be emancipated? In the second
case we give up the pretension of presenting something in
experience which corresponds to this term.[29]

In some details of phrasing – in its talk of a 'subject to be
emancipated' – this passage might seem true to its Kantian
lights and even to that critical 're-reading' of Marx that
Lyotard here recommends. But the postmodern scepticism shows up clearly in other, more decisive and
symptomatic ways. His nominalist language ('the term
"proletariat" ', 'the *name* of a subject') betokens Lyotard's
refusal to acknowledge that such words could possess any
reference outside the discourse of speculative reason. So it
is that the sublime does duty, yet again, as an analogue for
those strictly unrepresentable 'Ideas of Reason' whose
significance lies beyond the furthest bounds of conceptual
or experiential knowledge. For the only alternative – as
Lyotard would have it – is an Hegelian reading of Marx on
history according to which Ideas become incarnate in the
form of a universal class (the proletariat) whose advent
marks the definitive transcendence of all such ontological
distinctions.

This shows, to say the least, a somewhat limited grasp of
debates within the Marxist theoretical tradition since
Lukács's *History and Class-Consciousness*. And as a reading
of Kant it is even more skewed and tendentious, chiefly on
account of Lyotard's desire to aestheticize ethics and
politics by deploying the sublime as a figure of ultimate
heterogeneity, a wedge or a deconstructive lever that can
always be driven between the cognitive and evaluative
phrase-regimes. Such ideas thus serve to immaterialize the
language of any class-based social analysis or any account
of knowledge and human interests that would assign a
more than notional (speculative) content to terms like
'society' and 'class'. The whole line of argument bears a
striking rsemblance to other variations on the end-of-
ideology theme, among them Margaret Thatcher's
celebrated claim that 'society' doesn't exist, that 'individual'

interests, motives, or talents are the only ones that count, with the implication that talk of 'class' is just a tedious irrelevance in present-day social and economic terms. For whatever their express political allegiance – no matter how remote from the numbing banalities of Thatcherite rhetoric – these theorists must be seen as effectively endorsing the same ultra-nominal position.

It is here that postmodernism feeds back into the 'New Times' thinking of an otherwise shrewd and perceptive commentator like Stuart Hall. Such, after all, is the message implicit in his article on the 1992 election campaign and the reasons for Labour's defeat at the polls. If there is any way forward for socialism in the wake of this defeat then it clearly doesn't lie through the old left country of class politics, collective social values, or appeals to enlightened interest on the part of an informed and responsible electorate. Rather it must take full account of those factors – upward mobility, the 'classless society', free enterprise, individual 'empowerment' – whose appeal may be largely or wholly bogus when set against all the evidence to hand, but which have nonetheless managed to set the agenda for now and the foreseeable future. Such phrases have a ready-made suasive power, an ability to chime with the 'new sociology of aspirations', which leaves no room for the old left analysis. If words (styles of talk) are indeed all we have, and if those old language-games are now hopelessly outdated, then socialists had better move with the times and adapt their rhetoric accordingly.

Hall is not much given to philosophical excursions in the manner of Lyotard and kindred spirits on the postmodern cultural scene. But his view of current domestic political 'realities' has a good deal in common with that strain of nominalist thinking which claims a starting-point and justification in Kant's idea of the sublime. Thus the language of class, of real human interests or the 'subject to be emancipated' may still (for Lyotard or Hall) possess a certain ethical resonance, a power to evoke 'Ideas of Reason' whose meaning cannot be wholly exhausted by setbacks on the socialist road. But we shall be wrong – both agree – if we think that there is 'something experiential' that could ever 'correspond' to such ideas, or if we cling to the cognitivist illusion of 'presenting something in experience' that might actually bear them out. Now, of course, there is some truth in these arguments, both as a matter of social observation and (albeit more debatably) in so far as Lyotard would claim to derive them from a reading of the Kantian sublime. It can hardly be denied that class predicates (or socio-economic terms of analysis) become more difficult to apply – at least in any straightforward representationalist mode – at a time of rapid and complex demographic change when so many of the old class indicators no longer seem to have much purchase. To this extent Hall is fully justified in arguing that any workable socialist politics will need to take account of these factors when considering its future electoral strategy. And there is also a sense in which Lyotard is right to invoke Kant by way of controverting any simple correspondence theory of history, politics and class interests. Thus he can cite various passages in the third *Critique* which do indeed proffer the sublime as a token of the gulf between cognitive and evaluative phrase-regimes, of the existence of a 'suprasensible' realm beyond the bounds of phenomenal self-evidence, or of the confusions that arise when 'Ideas of Reason' are wrongly referred to the cognitive tribunal whose competence extends only to matters of theoretical understanding; that is, those cases where sensuous intuitions may be 'brought under' adequate concepts. In short, there are good reasons for maintaining that the interests of justice are not best served by a direct appeal to such interests as embodied in the actual experience of some existing class or group. Of course, one might well have arrived at this conclusion without the benefit of Lyotard's repeated and circuitous detours via Kant on the sublime. For Stuart Hall it is largely a matter of inductive observation, of remarking those current social trends and demographic shifts that pose a problem for more traditional (class-based) modes of analysis and critique. But for other theorists on the post-Marxist left there is a plausible (though by its very nature somewhat fugitive) connection to be drawn between the Kantian sublime and issues of a present-day political or socio-cultural import.[30]

Where this connection breaks down, as I have argued, is with the further move that presses such scepticism well beyond the point of an argued appeal to the evidence of demographic change. For it then becomes a pretext for the kind of wholesale nominalist approach that denies what should surely be apparent to any commentator, that is to say, the continuing *facts* of unemployment, social deprivation, unequal opportunities, two-tier health care, educational underprivilege and the rest. No doubt these data have then to be interpreted with a due regard to all the complicating factors – upward mobility, imaginary investment, Hall's 'new sociology of aspirations' – which will strike any reasonably sensitive observer of the current political scene. But there is little purpose in pursuing such analyses if they end up (like Lyotard's obsessive ruminations on the Kantian sublime) by denying both the relevance of class predicates and, beyond that, any version of the argument that would link those predicates – however nuanced or qualified – to the lived *experience* of class divisions in an unjust social order. It is for this reason, I would suggest, that the sublime has come to play such a prominent role in the thinking of postmodern culture-critics who are otherwise largely unconcerned with issues of a specialised philosophical nature. What it serves to promote, whether overtly or implicitly, is a sceptical ethos which simply takes for granted the collapse of all realist or representationalist paradigms, the advent of a postmodern 'hyperreality' devoid of ontological grounding or experiential content, and the need henceforth to abandon any thought of criticising social injustice from a standpoint of class solidarity based on communal perceptions and interests. In short, there is a strong elective affinity between this strain of post-Marxist/ 'New Times' thinking and the current high vogue for invocations of the Kantian sublime.

In his book *Protocols of Reading* Robert Scholes has some pertinent thoughts with regard to this issue of experience, class and representation as treated by various schools of poststructuralist theory.[31] His point, very briefly, is that critics cannot have it both ways: on the one hand proclaiming their 'radical' credentials and their concern with questions of politics, race, and gender while in the other adopting a nominalist (or 'textualist') stance which denies any possible ground of appeal in the realities of oppression as *known and experienced* by members of the relevant class, community, or interest-group. For theory then becomes just a play-off between different (incommensurable) language-games, an affair of multiple competing 'discourses' or 'subject-positions' devoid of any real-world consequence. Feminism, conversely, 'is based upon the notion of a gendered reader, and is driven by a perception of injustice in the relations between men and women in specific social, economic, and political terms'.[32] Scholes' main target here is the claim advanced by some (mostly male) critics: that since gender is after all a discursive product, a position constructed within language, or according to the rules 'arbitrarily' assigned by this or that set of cultural codes, *therefore* it must be possible for good-willed 'male feminists' to 'read as women', or adopt the kinds of viewpoint typically accorded to the female 'implied reader'. Such arguments understandably possess great appeal for theorists who would otherwise feel themselves *de facto* excluded from having anything relevant to say. But they are nonetheless mistaken, Scholes contends, since they ignore the manifold differences – the real and material (not just 'discursive') differences of interest – that characterize women's experience as subjects and readers.

This is not to say that males have nothing to learn from the encounter with feminist criticism or with work by women writers that foregrounds the issue of gender-role representation. Where the fallacy appears – as Elaine Showalter argues in her well-known essay on critical 'cross-dressing' – is with the notion that such roles go all the way down, so that male critics can somehow divest themselves of masculine attributes and espouse the other viewpoint through an act of readerly choice.[33] For this ignores the stubborn *facticity* of sexual difference, its inscription in a history (collective and individual) which cannot be so blithely transcended in pursuit of some notional view from elsewhere. As Scholes puts it:

> Both texts and readers are already written when they meet, but both may emerge from the encounter altered in some crucial respect. Feminist critics have made this semiotic process concrete and intelligible for us all, for gender – if not destiny – is one of those rough spots by which necessity, in the form of culture, grasps us and shapes our ends. Because women in this culture have been an underprivileged class, they have learned lessons in class consciousness that many men have not. Because it cuts across social class, gender brings the lessons of class consciousness into places normally so insulated by privilege as to be unconscious of the structure that supports and insulates them. Feminism, then, has drawn its strength from the ethical-political domain, by showing that women, as a class, have been regularly discriminated against by a cultural system that positions them as subordinate to men.[34]

This clear-headed passage is important to my argument for two connected reasons. First, it brings out the point that *difference* can only be a fashionable buzzword – like Lyotard's rhetoric of sublime 'heterogeneity' – so long as it is conceived in ideal abstraction from the contexts of real-world experience or the lived actualities of class and gender oppression. Second, it shows how such predicates of class-membership (in this case, 'women as a class') still play a vital descriptive and explanatory role, even – or especially – at times like the present when gender issues must be seen to 'cut across' other, more traditional modes of class analysis.

Scholes' argument here is partly a matter of empirical observation and partly, though he doesn't deploy such terms, the result of what amounts to a Kantian deduction on transcendental or *a priori* grounds. Thus practical experience is enough to confirm that any effective critique of social injustice, oppression and unequal opportunities will need to identify the particular groups whose lives, prospects or conditions of existence have been consequently damaged or curtailed. Such criticism may indeed come from non-members of the group, from male feminists who strive (so far as possible) to 'read as a woman', or from left intellectuals and cultural theorists who adopt a standpoint markedly at odds with their own class-interests narrowly conceived. Even so, they will be working on the prior assumption – *contra* the postmodern sceptics and nominalists – that such subordinate groups exist, that their names correspond (in however complex or overdetermined a way) to certain facts of shared or communicable human experience, and furthermore that criticism can best represent the interests of justice and truth by attempting to identify (and identify with) the experiences thus conveyed. At this point the empirical arguments join with the question as viewed under a Kantian (or 'conditions of possibility') aspect. For just as understanding (in its cognitive or theoretical mode) requires always that the manifold of sensuous intuitions be 'brought under' adequate concepts, so here it is the case that one cannot begin to grasp the lived realities of class or gender oppression without using terms (like 'gender' and 'class') which render that experience intelligible. And this holds despite all the problems of an empirical *and* a theoretical nature that are nowadays confronted by anyone seeking to apply such terms in a non-reductive or sufficiently 'flexible' manner.

One can therefore see why Scholes thinks it important to 'clarify the notion of *class*' as deployed in his argument, and to explain that the term is 'not restricted to socio-economic class, even though that remains as a central type of model for the concept'.[35] His point is not just that we need such enabling categories in order to wrest form from chaos, or to represent what would otherwise be lost to the flux of inchoate experience. More specifically, he is arguing *on ethico-political as well as on cognitive grounds* that we cannot do justice to these truths of experience – to the record of human suffering and waste brought about by various discriminatory practices – unless we acknowledge the applicability of class predicates in this wider sense. The problem about post-structuralism is that it denies the pertinence of all such categorical descriptions, and thus contrives to block the appeal to any kind of real-world knowledge or experience. For if everything is ultimately constructed in discourse – truth, reality, subject-positions, class allegiances – then *ex hypothese* we could only be deluded in thinking that any particular discourse (for instance, that of feminism) had a better claim to justice or truth than all the others currently on offer. And there is also a sense – a quite explicit and programmatic sense – in which post-structuralism works to undermine the very bases of critical or oppositional thought. That is to say, it takes the view (the nominalist view) that 'opposition' is itself just a product of discursive differentials, a term whose meaning inevitably fluctuates with the passage from one discourse to the next, and which therefore cannot be assigned any content (any real-world experiential truth) aside from its role in this or that (wholly conventional) signifying practice. And this applies not only to those aspects of inter-cultural linguistic difference (such as the various colour-term vocabularies or other such discrepant semantic fields) which post-structrualists often adduce in support of their claims for ontological relativity. Instances of this sort, though striking enough, need pose little problem for a theory of translation that views them as localised exceptions to be set against the broader regularities of human understanding within and across cultures.[36] But post-structuralism goes much further in its drive to relativise meaning and truth to the structures of linguistic representation or the force-field of contending discourses. For it operates on an abstract, quasi-systemic model of 'opposition' and 'difference' whereby those terms are deprived of all specific historical or experiential content, and treated, in effect, as linguistic artefacts or products of discursive definition.

Such is, of course, Saussure's account of language as a system of structural contrasts and differences 'without positive terms', a system that requires (among other preconditions for achieving theoretical consistency) the positing of an 'arbitrary' link between signifier and signified.[37] This explains his well-known lack of interest in the referential aspect of language, justified as a matter of working convenience or methodological priority. But there is no warrant whatsoever in Saussure for extending this strictly heuristic principle to the point where any mention of the referent – any appeal beyond the self-enclosed domain of signification – is regarded as a lapse into naive ('positivist' or 'metaphysical') ways of thought, to be dismissed briefly with a sigh.[38] What such ideas amount to is a form of specular misrecognition, a confinement to the structural-linguistic imaginary which mistakes its own theoretical preconceptions for the limits of language, thought, and experience in general. (Lacan is perhaps the most egregious example of the way that ontological distinctions – the imaginary, the symbolic, the real – can be so redefined as precisely to invert the order of relationship between them.)[39] Post-structuralism derives from this its dogged attachment to a nominalist thesis which treats the Saussurian 'arbitrary' sign – or the bar between signifier and signified – as a pretext for rejecting any notion that language might give access to the realm of cognitive or experiential knowledge.

It is at this point that some theorists have perceived a kinship with current readings of the Kantian sublime, a sense in which post-structuralism might be seen as engaged with the same problematic of radically disjunct or 'heterogeneous' discourses.[40] But in both cases such scepticism follows from a failure (or refusal) to grasp Kant's argument in the first *Critique* regarding the conceptually mediated character of all empirical truth-claims, or the requirement of 'bringing intuitions under concepts' in order to establish their cognitive validity. By ignoring this requirement, and instead switching their sights to the more seductive prospects of the Kantian sublime, these theorists end up with an aestheticised reading of Kant that reduces all forms of knowledge (and knowledge-constitutive interests) to the level of so many subject-positions constructed in and through language. It is worth quoting Scholes at some length here since he offers some particularly telling examples of the confusion

engendered by a textualist approach to issues of class- and
gender-politics.

> Readers who read as members of a class can be
> distinguished from those who are members of what Stanley
> Fish has called an 'interpretive community' ... in that
> membership in a class implies both necessity and interest.
> A member of the class *Jew* in Hitler's Germany or of the
> class *Black* in South Africa at present is a member of those
> classes by necessity and has an interest in the situation of
> the class as a whole ... A class, in this sense, is a cultural
> creation, part of a system of categories imposed upon all
> those who attain subjectivity in a given culture ... One may
> choose to be a feminist or not, but one is assigned one's
> gender and may change it only by extraordinary effort.
> The relationship between being female and being a
> feminist is neither simple nor to be taken for granted, but
> there is no comparable relationship between being a
> deconstructionist and belonging to a class – which is of
> course not to say that deconstruction is free of interest or
> beyond ideology ... A feminist literary critic writes for
> other critics, to be sure, but she also writes on behalf of
> other women and, as a critic, she is strengthened by the
> consciousness of this responsibility. A male critic, on the
> other hand, may work within the feminist paradigm but
> never be a fully-fledged member of the class of feminists.[41]

My one minor quarrel has to do with Scholes' idea that
deconstruction is chiefly to blame for dissolving those
various categories – especially the interlinked concepts of
class membership and cognitive representation – which
alone make it possible to render such experience
intelligible. In fact, one could say more accurately (at least
with reference to Derrida's work) that deconstruction
continues to operate with those concepts and respect their
rigorous necessity, while at the same time resisting any
premature appeal to the binary structures (or logics of
exclusion) on which they customarily depend.[42] This is not
to deny that there are some texts of Derrida that do lend
credence to Scholes' charge. Among them are those essays
where he touches on the topic of sexual difference and the
imagined possibility of 'reading as a woman', or exploring

all manner of polymorphous gender-roles, as a strategy for contesting received ('phallogocentric') discourses of meaning and truth.[43] But in the bulk of his more considered and analytical work, Derrida is at pains to disavow any notion that difference – as a concept and a fact of experience – can be somehow transformed through the utopian 'freeplay' of a writing that blithely rejects such irksome constraints. Scholes' criticism applies more justly to that facile strain of postmodern and post-structuralist thought which takes it as read – with no philosophical qualms – that truth *just is* what we are given to make of it according to various textual strategies, gender-role constructs, and signifying practices. In which case it would follow (logically, though absurdly) that 'there is no significant difference between reading about an experience and having an experience, because experience never simply occurs.'[44]

The switch from 'never simply' to 'simply never' – from deconstruction to postmodernism, or Derrida to Baudrillard – is one that occurs with remarkable ease among thinkers of a 'New Times' persuasion. This is why it is important to address some of the muddles and misreadings (especially misreadings of Kant) that currently exert such widespread appeal. For these issues have a relevance outside and beyond the specialised enclaves of cultural and critical theory. In fact, they are within reach of the single most urgent question now confronting left thinkers in Britain and the United States; namely, what remains of the socialist project at a time when distorted consensus values have gone so far towards setting the agenda for 'informed' or 'realistic' political debate. It might seem extravagant – just a piece of academic wishful thinking – to make such claims for the importance of getting Kant right on the relation between epistemology, ethics and aesthetics, or for pursuing the question 'What Is Enlightenment?' as raised once more in Foucault's late writings on the politics of truth.[45] But for better or worse it has been largely in the context of 'theory' – that capacious though ill-defined genre – that these issues have received their most intensive scrutiny over the past two decades. It is unfortunate that so much of this debate has been characterised by a proneness to the vagaries of Francophile intellectual fashion, as well as by a skewed and superficial grasp of its own formative prehistory. Philosophical confusions can often go along with disastrous failures of political judgment, as recent cases (Heidegger's among them) have demonstrated plainly enough. All of which tends to support the idea that postmodernism is more a symptom of the present malaise than a cure for modernity and its manifold discontents.

Notes

[1] Christopher Norris, *Uncritical Theory: Postmodernism, Intellectuals and the Gulf War*, Lawrence & Wishart, London 1992.
[2] Francis Fukuyama, 'The End of History', *The National Interest*, Washington DC 1989. See also Fukuyama, *The End of History and the Last Man*, Hamish Hamilton, London 1992.
[3] Fukuyama, 'Changed Days for Ruritania's Dictator', *The Guardian*, 8 April 1991.
[4] Norris, *op cit*, p 156.
[5] See, for instance, Jonathan Steele, Edward Mortimer and Gareth Stedman Jones, 'The End of History?' (a discussion of Fukuyama's essay), in *Marxism Today*, November 1989, pp 26-33.
[6] See the essays collected in Stuart Hall and Martin Jacques (eds), *New Times: The Changing Face of Politics in the 1990s*, Lawrence & Wishart, London 1989.
[7] Stuart Hall, 'No New Vision, No New Votes', *New Statesman & Society*, 17 April 1992, pp 14-15. This issue also carried a number of other 'post-mortem' articles on the reasons for Labour's electoral defeat and the best way forward for British socialism.
[8] *Ibid.*
[9] See Raymond Williams, *Keywords: A Vocabulary of Culture and Society*, Fontana, London 1976.
[10] See, for instance, Jean Baudrillard, *Selected Writings*, Mark Poster (ed), Polity Press, Cambridge 1989; also *America*, Verso, London 1988, *Fatal Strategies*, Pluto Press, London 1989 and *Revenge of the Crystal: A Baudrillard Reader*, Pluto Press, London 1990.
[12] Stuart Hall, *op cit.*
[12] *Ibid.*
[13] *Ibid.*
[14] Antonio Gramsci, *Selections from the Prison Notebooks*, ed. and trans. Quintin Hoare and Geoffrey Nowell Smith, Lawrence & Wishart, London 1971.
[15] Terry Eagleton, *Ideology: An Introduction*, Verso, London 1991, p 3.

[16] *Ibid*, p 4.

[17] See, for instance, Peter de Bolla, *The Discourse of the Sublime: Readings in History, Aesthetics and the Subject*, Basil Blackwell, Oxford 1989; Neil Hertz, *The End of the Line: Essays on Psychoanalysis and the Sublime*, Columbia University Press, New York 1985; Hugh Silverman (ed), *The Textual Sublime*, State University of New York Press, Alvany, NY 1990; and Slavoj Žižek, *The Sublime Object of Ideology*, Verso, London 1990.

[18] See Jean-Francois Lyotard, *The Differend: Phrases in Dispute*, trans. Georges van den Abbeele, Manchester University Press, Manchester 1988; also *The Inhuman Reflections on Time*, trans. Geoffrey Bennington and Rachel Bowlby, Polity Press, Cambridge 1991.

[19] Immanuel Kant, *Critique of Pure Reason*, trans. N. Kemp Smith, Macmillan, London 1933; *Critique of Practical Reason*, trans. Lewis W. Beck, Bobbs-Merrill, Indianapolis 1977; and *Critique of Judgment*, trans. J.C. Meredith, Clarendon Press, Oxford 1978.

[20] Saul Kripke, *Naming and Necessity*, Basil Blackwell, Oxford 1980.

[21] See Lyotard, *The Differend, op cit*, p 179.

[22] *Ibid*, p 19.

[23] *Ibid*, p 9.

[24] *Ibid*, p 19.

[25] For a sustained and intelligent (if far from conclusive) address to these issues, see Tony Bennett, *Outside Literature*, Routledge, London 1990; also the essays collected in Derek Attridge, Geoff Bennington and Robert Young (eds), *Post-Structuralism and the Questions of History*, Cambridge University Press, Cambridge 1987.

[26] Stephen Greenblatt, 'Resonance and Wonder', in *Learning to Curse: Essays in Early Modern Culture*, Routledge, London 1990, pp 161-83.

[27] Lyotard, *The Differend, op cit*, p 148.

[28] *Ibid*, p 13.

[29] Lyotard, 'Complexity and the Sublime', in Lisa Appignanesi (ed), *Postmodernism*, ICA Documents/Free Association Books, London 1989, pp 19-26, p 23.

[30] See, for instance, Dick Hebdige, 'The Impossible Object: Towards a Sociology of the Sublime', *New Formations*, no. 1, Spring 1987, pp 47-76; and *Hiding in the Light: On Images and Things*, Routledge, London 1988.

[31] Robert Scholes, *Protocols of Reading*, Yale University Press, New Haven 1989. For a wide-ranging treatment of these issues from a socio-philosophical viewpoint, see Margaret Gilbert, *On Social Facts*, Routledge, London 1989.

[32] Scholes, *Protocols of Reading, op cit*, p 91.

[33] Elaine Showalter, 'Critical Cross-Dressing', *Raritan*, vol. 3, no. 2, Fall 1983, pp 130-49. See also Marjorie Garber, *Vested Interests: Cross-Dressing and Cultural Anxiety*, Routledge, New York & London 1992; Stephen Heath, *The Sexual Fix*, Macmillan, London 1982; Mary Jacobus, 'Reading Woman (Reading)' and 'The Difference of View', in *Reading Woman: Essays in Feminist Criticism*, Columbia University Press, New York 1986, pp 3-24 and 27-40; and Alice Jardine and Paul Smith (eds),

Men in Feminism, Methuen, London 1987.

[34] Scholes, *op cit*, p 92.

[35] *Ibid*, p 92.

[36] For further discussion of this and related topics, see especially W.V.O. Quine, *'Ontological Relativity' and Other Essays*, Columbia University Press, New York 1969, and Donald Davidson, *Inquiries into Truth and Interpretation*, Clarendon Press, Oxford 1984.

[37] Ferdinand de Saussure, *Course in General Linguistics*, trans. Wade Baskin, Fontana, London 1974; also translated by Roy Harris (Open Court, La Salle, Ill. 1986) with significant changes of terminology and detail.

[38] For a vigorously argued critique of these ideas, see Raymond Tallis, *Not Saussure*, Macmillan, London 1988. There is also some useful commentary to be found in Jonathan Culler, *Saussure*, Fontana, London 1976; Roy Harris, *Reading Saussure*, Duckworth, London 1987; and David Holdcraft, *Saussure: Signs, Systems and Arbitrariness*, Cambridge University Press, Cambridge 1991.

[39] See Jacques Lacan, *Ecrits: A Selection*, trans. Alan Sheridan, Tavistock, London 1977.

[40] See, for instance, Hebdige, *Hiding in the Light*; Hertz, *The End of the Line*; Silverman (ed), *The Textual Sublime*; and Žižek, *The Sublime Object of Ideology*, *op cit*.

[41] Scholes, *op cit*, pp 92-3.

[42] See especially Jacques Derrida, 'Afterword: Toward an Ethics of Discussion', in *Limited Inc.* (2nd edn) Northwestern University Press, Evanston, Ill. 1988, pp 111-60.

[42] See, for instance, Derrida, 'Women in the Beehive: A Seminar With Jacques Derrida', in Jardine and Smith (eds), *Men in Feminism*, *op cit*, pp 180-203.

[44] Scholes, *op cit*, p 99.

[45] See Michel Foucault, 'What is Enlightenment?', in Paul Rabinow (ed), *The Foucault Reader*, Penguin, Harmondsworth 1984, pp 32-50.

Rediscovering Values

JEFFREY WEEKS

Values, Whose Values?

We live, breathe and excrete values, writes Fekete. 'Yet it is no exaggeration to say that the oceans and continents of value, though much travelled remain almost uncharted in anyway suitable for the navigational contingencies of postmodern itineraries'.[1]

This underlines a crucial issue. We are besieged by value debates. The last decade or so has seen a torrent of value-laden arguments, largely from the political and moral right, but also from popes and preachers, ayotollahs, religious revivalists and fundamentalists of various political hues, which tell us unrelentingly how we should live, and whose protagonists do their best to ensure that we conform to their strictures. Yet the overwhelming feeling in our culture is of moral confusion rather than moral certainty. The 'fashionable madmen', as W.H. Auden called them, parade their fantasies of a final reconciliation between our desires and their will, yet we actually live with a confusing plurality of values, some particularist, some claiming a universal validity, but each rooted in different traditions, histories and theoretical and political trajectories, and many of them in stark contradiction, one to the other.

The central argument of this essay is that we must start rethinking values by exploring, not rejecting that plurality. Rather than imposing an artificial order on moral confusion, we need to learn how to negotiate the hazards of social complexity and moral diversity. It is sometimes said that the contemporary progressive agenda lacks a unifying 'vision', which can bind disparate needs and aspirations into a coherent end project. Yet, I suggest, new visions of a glorious, transcendent future are what have led us astray, whether it is the vision of a personal 'liberation' or of the redemption of social life in a new, and higher type of civilisation. Instead, we need to clarify our values, in their multiplicity and plurality. We can only negotiate the oceans and continents of value if we first chart their heterogeneity.

On a group of theories, David McLellan has argued, one can found a school. But on a group of values 'one can found a culture, a civilisation, a new way of living together'.[2] For speaking of values is a way of describing the sort of life we want to lead, or think we should lead.[3] Values provide a series of principles from which we can try to deduce goals, and then develop policies. Values help us to clarify what we believe to be right or wrong, permissible and impermissible. They should also, in a complex and pluralistic world, help us to ensure that what we think is right is not necessarily what other people think is right, and to resolve differences in a democratic fashion.

Diversity and democracy therefore provide major foci of my argument, and set the parameters for what follows. These are potent yet ambiguous terms, for their meanings change as the world changes, and as needs and desires change with it. At the centre of my own perspective is a belief that it is wrong to seek the 'truth' of values, ethics and morality either in history, theory, science, or some extra-terrestial source. On the contrary we constantly invent or re-invent moralities as we face the contingencies of the present and the veiled landmarks of the future. This makes talking about values peculiarly hazardous.

Inventing Moralities

Let's look a little more closely at the problem of 'invention'. Michel Foucault observed towards the end of his life that:

> What is good, is something that comes through innovation.
> The good does not exist, like that, in an atemporal sky,
> with people who would be like the Astrologers of the Good,

whose job is to determine what is the favorable nature of
the stars. The good is defined by us, it is practised, it is
invented. And this is a collective work.[4]

We can draw from this at least two useful ideas, certainly
not new nor original, but succinctly summarised. First of
all, there is the emphasis on the idea of the 'good' as a
human creation, not a gift from science, or an imposition
from without (though of course, it can be presented as the
first, and can become the second). Secondly, there is the
emphasis on the collective origins of our notions of the
'good'. They are not simply emanations of the minds of
philosophers. They are given meaning, and validated by
traditions of belief and practice, reviewed, reconstructed
and invented through collective experience. And as there
are many traditions and collectivities, so there are many
notions of the 'good'.

The context in which Foucault made this comment is
illuminating. It is taken from an interview he gave at the
University of California at Berkeley towards the end of his
life, and is important because it signals a crucial moment in
the work of a thinker generally associated with postmodernist critiques. (Whether that is a just description of
Foucault's work is another matter.) His discussion of the
basis of morals represents, I would argue, a shift from
'deconstruction' to what we can, for want of a better term,
call 'reconstruction', a move from usefully tearing apart
the presuppositions of western thought to reveal their
(often dubious) origins and multiple meanings, to
beginning the arduous task of rethinking, what Stuart Hall
in a different, but related, context, has called the 'hard
road to renewal'.[5]

A major factor in the intellectual revolution of the past
twenty years has been the challenge to 'essentialism' in
critical thinking, which has sought to undermine the idea
that 'society', 'culture', 'history', or any other hypostasised
entity, has an inner essence of truth from which the
validity of their structures may be deduced. In areas such
as sexuality and gender, as well as in broader fields of
political and social analysis, it has given rise to a

transformation of the ways we conceive of the past and the historic present in which we live. Anti-essentialist arguments have demonstrated that the constructs and divisions we take for granted as 'natural' and inevitable are in fact historical and contingent. The hope of every ideology, Hall has suggested, 'is to naturalise itself out of History into Nature, and thus to become invisible, to operate unconsciously'.[6] The anti-essentialist critique has attempted to lay bare the bones of this naturalising exercise, and revealed the complex histories which have constructed our ideas of the social, the sexual, and even nature itself.

But critiques of essentialist modes of thought do not answer, but pose afresh, questions of value. If there is no foundation in nature, science or history for the truth claims of our belief systems, where, in our pluralistic universe, can truth or validity lie? In the hallowed phrase, if God (any God, even a secular simulacrum) is dead, is anything permitted?

Certain strands of post-modernist writing have in fact surrendered to nihilism or a celebration of consumerist amorality, tendencies which have in turn been seen as defining features of postmodernism. My own argument is that this need not be the case. There are countless traditions with clearly defined values, which may be 'invented', but provide nonetheless valid guides for living. The problem does not lie in the absence of values, but in our inability to recognise that there are many different ways of being human, and in articulating the common strands which often unite them.

The American philosopher Michael Walzer has explored the problem of 'invention' in some depth.[7] He distinguishes what he terms the 'path of invention' from two other tendencies in moral philosophy, the 'path of discovery' and the 'path of interpretation'.

The 'path of discovery' assumes that moral principles are out there, somewhere in the heavens or nature, waiting to be discovered by detached and dispassionate philosophers. But philosophers, as we know, have a tendency not to agree, and while some have offered a militant dogmatism others have during this century either retreated into the arcane micro-philosophy of linguistic analysis, or militantly abstained from the search for truth altogether. Walzer would concur with this abstentionism. The search for the truth of morality, he argues, ignores the fact that the everyday world *is* a moral world, and 'we would do better to study its internal rules, maxims, contentions, and ideals, rather than detach ourselves from it in search of a universal and transcendent standpoint'.[8] This is his preferred 'path of interpretation'.

Discovery is not necessary, Walzer suggests, because we already have what the discoverers claim to find: we already live in a moral world. The task of the 'connected' moral critic is to evoke the shared moral values, by telling a 'plausible story' about which values ought to be fundamental.[9] These values may have been invented in the past, but are now embedded in thick communal traditions.

The problem of invented traditions, Walzer goes on, is that they make truths, they seek to provide what God and Nature unaccountably forgot to provide, a universal corrective for all the different social moralities. They have attempted to provide a goal, an end, whether justice, political virtue, or goodness, or some other truth, which have demanded the bending of human wills, energies and desires into a preconceived ideal, where unorthodoxy or resistance have been the ultimate sins. The results, whether (to take just two of the most obvious examples) in the terror waged by the most ardent advocates of the French revolutionary morality, or in the enthusiasm to make 'homo Sovieticus', the 'new Soviet man' in the wake of the 1917 Russian revolution, have been universally disastrous.

So a moral code or value system, invented by others for our own good, must be avoided at all costs. But that leaves room for asking whether the term 'invention' in a weaker sense may not be of some value. As Walzer concedes, the weak sense of invention comes close to his own preferred approach of interpretation and connectedness. It stresses the importance of human creativity, of basing values in lived experience, and of exploring the variety of human possibilities already apparent to us. As Laclau has put it, 'If the word of God can no longer be heard, we can start giving our own voices a new dignity'.[10]

Here lies the relevance of addressing the significance of the new social movements, increasingly dispersed, as Enzensberger has put it, throughout social life.[11] Giddens, for example, has urged us to recognise the importance of the new movements, and the elective communities they have given rise to, in generating what he calls a 'life politics'.[12] It is in these movements, around sexuality and gender, race, the environment, and so on, that we can actually witness the constant invention and reinvention of values. The new movements have been, in Melucci's graphic phrase, social laboratories where new lifestyles are shaped and tested.[13] They have offered (to echo John Stuart Mill's famous comment) 'experiments in living',[14] experiments, however, by individuals which are given context and meaning through collective experience.

These new 'invented moralities' are not, of course, free from their own conflicts, contradictions and even petty tyrannies. But they do embody attempts to go beyond the nihilism and amorality of the postmodern condition. In place of a single master-narrative, they often embody attempts to shape meaningful micro-narratives. The existential choice, the new movements seem to confirm, only makes sense in and through our sense of collective belongings.

The new social movements offer one set of examples of the ways in which values are constantly being rein-terpreted, renegotiated, invented or reinvented in the contemporary world. The difficulties lie not in the sense of belonging that they embody, but in finding means of ensuring that the particular allegiances we make can co-reside with the equally resonant allegiances and claims of other traditions and communities. Connectedness, yes. But it also seems imperative that we develop a sense of belonging as members of the wider human community: to invent or reinvent not only particular but universal solidarities. So, if the relationship between diversity and democracy provides one pole of my concerns, the linked tensions between the relative and the universal provides another. The key issue is whether it is possible to find a common normative standard by which we can come to terms with different ways of life, whether we can balance relativism with some sense of minimum universal values.

Radical Humanism

Ernesto Laclau has argued that the first condition of a radically democratic society 'is to accept the contingent and radically open character of all its values – and in that sense, to abandon the aspiration to a single foundation'.[15] That does not mean that it is impossible to develop convincing value systems. What it does entail, however, is that we are open and honest about the basis on which we establish our moral and political projects.

If, like Laclau, we espouse the values of a radically democratised and plural society, within a broader perspective of 'radical humanism', we must justify them not through the metaphysical but through argument and debate, by exploring their likely effects in achieving what I take to be the overriding goals, enhancing life opportunities and liberty. Morality, as Michael Walzer has said, 'is something we have to argue about'. There is no final end, no final proof of what is right or wrong – only the possibility of continuing debate about it.[16] But that position already contains a moral viewpoint and project: a commitment precisely to the values of open discussion and the free play of argument – what Bauman calls 'the art of civilised conversation' between and across cultural traditions.[17]

As this suggests, of course, there are many potential moral projects. As the 'juggernaut of modernity' gathers speed towards some postmodern future, the question of 'how shall we live' becomes even more fraught, and has to be answered by day to day decisions about how to behave, what to wear, what to eat, and so on.[18] In responding to such apparently mundane but potent questions, we inevitably draw on the values of the traditions, commu-

nities and moral projects we align ourselves with. Which
we choose is not pregiven. Choices are determined by a
host of factors, some individual, some collective. Choice is
not absolutely free; it is shaped by history, and the
complex relations of domination and subordination that
circumscribe individual life chances.

The commitment to a form of radical humanism is
therefore one shaped by many histories, and is one choice
among many. Its validity cannot depend on any *a priori*
arguments, though it can justifiably draw on what
historical evidence for its case there is. In the end, as a
moral project, it will stand or fall on its ability to convince
people that it will achieve certain desirable ends.

These ends embrace a paradox: respect for difference,
and the affirmation of human solidarity. The paradox is
real in one sense, because the assertion of different ways of
being apparently fragments any unitary project, opening
the way to a cacophony of different claims and aspirations.
But if we look at the claims of the different communities
from another position we can perhaps begin to dissolve
the paradox, though not eliminate the difficulties. For the
claim that there are different ways of being human can
itself become a constituent element of a humanistic
project, defining the human as precisely concerning
respect for difference. Human solidarity thus becomes a
project not of realising what already is there, undiscovered
beneath our noses, but of constructing bonds across the
chasm of difference. The task of radical humanism then
becomes the making of a human community which is a
community of communities. Difference is relativised as part
of the making of certain universal principles. At the same
time, the universal is itself relativised, becoming not an
unproblematic given but an articulation of a variety of
social discourses and logics around an evolving project.

They key term, I would argue, is 'community'.
Community has no specific political belonging. It has its
liberal interpretation as well as organic conservative and
socialistic. For Jeremy Bentham, the philosopher of
utilitarianism, the community was a fictitious body,

composed of the individual persons who are considered as
constituting as it were its members. The interest of the
community is then, what? – the sum of the several
members who compose it.[19]

Recently the stark utilitarianism of such thinking has been
challenged in liberal political theory. The idea of
community has developed a strong resonance as a focus
for dissatisfaction with personal existence under liberalism: a revulsion at its coldness, impersonality, instrument-
alism and narrow self-interest. Community becomes
important here as an 'escape from abstract personhood'.[20]
It provides instead a solid basis for social and political
commitment.

The renewed interest in communitarian thinking stems
from a belief that liberal individualism is a major cause of
the growing lack of social cohesion in western societies.
For Alasdair MacIntyre, the triumph of liberalism, an
ideology which presents itself as the truth of human
existence while itself having clear conditions of existence,
and the collapse of the Aristotlean concept of man as
having a shared good, has brought us to the edge of a new
Dark Age.[21] The neo-conservative theorist Daniel Bell
laments the 'loss of *civitas*', the spontaneous willingness to
honour the city of which one is a member.[22] The result is a
fragmented society, dominated by possessive individualism.

Communitarian thinkers see society as more than a
collection of atomistic individuals bound together by self
interest and the pursuit of individually defined goods; it is
made up of different communities which are based on
ideas of reciprocity and mutual obligation. In asserting
this they are able to call on a long, half buried tradition in
social and political thought. On the one hand there is the
civic republican tradition of politics, which had its origins
in Greek and Roman thought, and achieved its apotheosis
in the Italian city states of the Renaissance and in the ideals
of early American republicanism. It stressed membership,
active citizenship, and civic responsibility. On the other
hand there is the tradition, particularly strong in British

social thought, of moral critique of utilitarian capitalism, and of socialist thinking which stressed against it the strength of community. This is the tradition that Raymond Williams has reconstructed in *Culture and Society*, and includes such disparate writers as Thomas Carlyle, John Ruskin, William Morris, Guild Socialists like G.D.H. Cole, and R.H. Tawney.[23] This is a 'great tradition' of communitarian writing which has provided a counter-culture to the dominant political practices (of both left and right) of the twentieth century.

The new social movements are heirs to these traditions. The communitarianism of the movements, and the communities of identity they simultaneously give rise to and grow out of, is thus not a bolt from the blue but part of an important tradition in political thought and practice. The key element is the belief that individuals do not simply choose community as a desirable end, but that individual identities are in large part constituted by communities, which in turn individuals must discover and realise.[24]

By definition, however, communities are not fixed once and for all. They change as the arguments which shape them over time continue, and as other communities exercise their gravitational pull. For community, as Bauman says, is 'first and foremost a project, a strategy, a declaration of intention and the action which follows it'.[25] The social relations of a community are repositories of meaning for its members, not sets of mechanical linkages between isolated individuals. A community offers a 'vocabulary of values' through which individuals construct their understanding of the social world, and of their sense of identity and belonging.[26]

So if community is constitutive, it is also imagined, in the sense used by Anderson in his study of invented, but still potently mobilising nationalisms.[27] The idea of community has different meanings for its members, depending on their own outlooks, experiences and allegiances. For communities come in many shapes and sizes, ranging from the geographically fixed to the communities of identity around sexuality, which are rarely related to a fixed space. Communities can continue over many generations, sustained by material interests and a passionate history of resistance. Or they can be communities of affect around rock music, humanitarian groupings such as Band Aid and other movements of international solidarity.

To survive, a community must be constantly re-imagined, sustained over time by common practices and symbolic re-enactments which reaffirm both identity and difference. A national community may be sustained by allegiance to the flag, national days, the ritual of elections, or monarchy, by victories in war, war memorials and military pride, or by the less harmful ephemeral hysteria of athletic competitions or the soccer World Cup. A black community may re-enact its difference through defence of its territory against racist attacks or the symbolic presence of the police. But it may also celebrate it in carnival, the inversion of the daily humdrum existence where reality is turned upside down, the streets become the property of the oppressed, and the repressed experiences of the community can return, triumphantly for the day. Or the losses of the AIDS community can be mourned, the lives of the dead validated, and the resilience and creativity of the living affirmed, through candle-lit vigils and the sewing of memorial quilts.

Without such re-imaginings a community will die, or become meaningless before the onrush of history.

'Humanity', in the sense of the unity of the species, may be seen as yet another community, though one that the social struggles and upheavals of the past two and a half centuries (the period of 'modernity') has given a special meaning.[28] The challenge is to construct that unity in a way which achieves ('invents' or 'imagines') a sense of 'universal human values' while respecting human variety and difference. Like the shaping of particularist communities, this is a moral and political project, but one given urgency by the complex processes of globalisation (of risk and threat, *and* of opportunity) that constitutes the modern world.

The task of the radical humanist project, then, is to tease

out of the multiple forms of difference, rooted in contingency and a radical historicity, those common strands which can make the 'human bond'. This is not to reject the traditions of post-Enlightenment humanism *tout court*, but it does require a recognition of the historical traditions which led to its emergence, and of the often murky origins of many of its key elements: its ethnocentrism while claiming a universal validity, its conjuring up of a universal 'Manhood' which systematically excluded women. Humanity is not an essence to be realised, but a pragmatic construction, a perspective, to be developed through the articulation of the variety of individual projects, of differences, which constitute our humanity in the broadest sense.

Living with Difference

There are of course hazards in this. 'Community' is often used to preserve and re-invent our differences, to protect our individual and collective diversity. This is a necessary part of living in a complex world. There is a danger, however, that diversity can be constructed as absolute difference. This is most acutely signalled by the potency of nationalism in the modern world. Nationalism has proved a powerful force, for good and ill. In the struggles of colonised peoples against the metropolitan state it has proved an engine for dismantling the old world empires, and for the achievement of national autonomy and pride. Its energy has fatally undermined the old transnational empire of the Czars and the Bolsheviks, and threatened the unitary nature even of the oldest nation states, as in Spain or Britain. But, Janus-like, it also has behind it the wars of the twentieth century, and ahead of it the fragmentation of the post-colonial states, as the logic of nationalism, in India, Pakistan, Sri Lanka, Yugoslavia, Nigeria, Ethiopia, and many other countries, re-defines the nation into ever neater national identities, based on ancient or re-imagined tribal, ethnic or racial divides.

As Paul Gilroy has argued, 'The discourses of nation and people are saturated with racial connotations.'[29] Even as the ancient nation states of western Europe come together, albeit with many difficulties, to form the first 'post-national state', where old enmities are transcended by a new sense of common purpose, there are dangerous signs that this could be at the expense of the non-European peoples who have provided the migrant labour without which the renewed prosperity of the west could not have happened.

The absolutisation of difference, however, is not confined to the older movements, like nationalism. It is an ever present danger in the new movements, and the communities they have grown out of. This has been vividly illustrated in recent decades by the development of what has been described as 'category politics', in which political mobilisation on the basis of the militant assertion of difference by self-defined groups became the basis on which needs were defined by the local state. As Mercer has described, with specific reference to one example of a political discourse which flirted with identity-politics, that of the Greater London Council in the 1980s:

> expectations about equal participation and representation in decision-making were converted into sectional demands and competing claims about the legitimation of different needs. The possibility of coalitions was pre-empted by the competitive dynamic of who would have priority access to resources.[30]

The difficulty lies in an identity politics which assumes the essentialist nature of identity and difference, and a hierarchy of racial, sexual or gendered oppressions. A paradox lies at the heart of this form of politics. On the one hand, there is the felt need to assert publicly and privately a strong sense of self, rooted in particular histories, cultures and languages, which allows the articulation of diverse identities. The problem here lies in how the boundaries between the different identities should be drawn, and who can speak for them. Are the elders of the black communities more entitled to speak for community values than the black feminists who challenge them? On the other, there is the ever-present danger of a politics entirely rooted in particular experiences, which all too readily gives rise to a self-righteous assertion that if one inhabits a certain identity this gives one the right to pressure others into particular ways of behaving.[31]

As Paul Gilroy has argued:

> Unable to control the social relations in which they find themselves, people have shrunk the world to the size of their communities and begun to act politically on that basis.[32]

The result has been the development of a variety of pseudo pluralisms in which difference became a substitute for any wider sense of solidarity. The danger lies not in the commitments to community and difference, but in their exclusive nature. A particular community all too often becomes the focus of retreat from the challenges of modernity, while identity becomes a fixed attribute to hold on to at all costs. Yet, as Sandel suggests:

> Each of us moves in an indefinite number of communities, some more inclusive than others, each making different claims on our allegiance, and there is no saying in advance which is *the* society or community whose purpose should govern the disposition of any particular set of our attributes and endowments.[33]

We may be black *and* gay, women *and* disabled, Welsh *and* British *and* European *and* citizens of spaceship earth, and these may give rise to 'conflicting social obligations' as we weigh our loyalties and allegiances. These conflicts are played out in each individual, and can give rise to acute conflicts in the communities themselves. They also, however, provide the opportunity for creativity and choice, for the advancement of autonomy, and for the building of an ever wider sense of community.

For difference can never be absolute, nor identities finally fixed in the modern world. We need to proceed, as Stuart Hall has argued, 'by the recognition of a necessary heterogeneity and diversity; by a concept of "identity" which lives with and through, not despite, difference; by *hybridity*.'[34]

Hybridity is a marked feature of all our identities in the world of late or postmodernity. Identity is not a finished product, but a process, which is never finally achieved, or completed. The fluidity of identities, and the diversity they reflect, provides the terrain of modern value debates. To see identity and community as fixed and eternal leads to political deadlock. To see them as multiple and open provides a space in which change becomes possible.

Solidarity and Difference

In the absence of a common language for dealing with the dialectic of difference and solidarity, two types of argument have typically emerged. The first is the 'discourse of rights', probably still the most powerful mobilising force in the world of politics and morals. In the USA the protection of individual rights is enshrined in the constitution, and the claim to individual and minority rights has become the basis of some of the most significant and transforming currents in contemporary politics, from the civil rights and black power movements, to modern social movements. Elsewhere in the west, a rights-based politics is similarly entrenched in written constitutions, bills of rights and constitutional courts – though not in Britain, where a rights-based tradition is enfeebled.

Unfortunately, the claim to right does not easily tell us whose rights are to be respected. The claim that there are universal human rights illustrates the dilemma. Article 2 of the United Nations Declaration of Human Rights in 1948 claimed that everyone is entitled to certain rights and freedoms irrespective of race, colour, sex, language, religion, politics, national or social origins, property, birth, and other status. This was intended as having a universal validity. Yet the language and terms are clearly rooted in the norms (if not always the practices) of liberal-democratic, highly industrialised countries. As such, the Declaration, implicitly calls on all nations to become such societies.[35]

The Declaration has had, not surprisingly, a chequered history. Despite their universal claims, these apparently global rights were neither universally accepted, nor were they always interpreted consistently. They became both a stick with which to encourage developing countries, and a weapon in the Cold War against the unreformed Soviet Union and its allies, though less so in the case of the People's Republic of China after its great rapprochment with the USA, and even less so in the case of those 'authoritarian regimes' that publicly allied with the west.

After the collapse of international communism, and the democratic surge after 1989, with the promised triumph of liberal democracy and the postulated 'end of history' (a history which has, nevertheless reasserted itself with a vengeance), it may well seem that this awkward history may radically change. But given the reflex action against western values represented by a resurgent nationalism and the universalising claims of militant Islam, we can still doubt whether the universal rights set forth in 1948 have any greater resonance now than before.

More useful than a paper declaration, however valuable, would be a set of universal minimum standards rooted both in an empirical universality, and in the concerns of every parish, as Walzer puts it.[36] The fundamental issue is whether it is possible to articulate a minimum universal standard, the basis of a community of humankind, which recognises that there are some acts condemned in one society which also breach the codes of all societies; while accepting that there may well be different ways of acting out and living that standard.

Agnes Heller has confronted this question by proposing what she calls an 'incomplete ethico-political concept of justice' which seeks to establish 'common normative foundations for different ways of life'.[37] Such a concept would not presuppose any particular social system as the good or the just one. It would not seek to mould different ways of life into a single 'ideal' pattern. It proposes, on the contrary, the existence of a variety of ways of life bound together by ties of 'symmetric reciprocity'.

The acceptance of a minimum standard is dependent, then, on the acceptance by different cultures that they have certain norms in common, and that they are equalised by common norms.

This directs us to the second major tradition concerned with universalising demands, the discourse of emancipation. Its roots are deeply entrenched in the struggles of early modernity against the dead weight of tradition, which blocked individual autonomy and certain basic freedoms, for example of religious observance. Over the past two centuries it has become the rallying call against economic exploitation, and the various forms of oppression, of class, race, colonialism, gender, sexuality. Even more powerfully than the discourse of rights, this has proved a strong mobilising force.[38] The emancipatory discourse offers a vision of a totally free society, where everyone's potential is fully realised. As the politics of liberation, it shaped the ideals and rhetoric of the social movements of the 1960s and 1970s that were most concerned with re-ordering the personal sphere.

The problem is that the 'emancipatory potential' of the various movements which claim the name is not always self evident. There have been fierce conflicts over the meaning of emancipation. More often than not, the emancipatory movements have succeeded in making their voices heard in so far as they represent the militant particularism of some, rather than a social emancipation for all. More disturbing still has been the claims of such movements that they represent the privileged agents of change, whether those agents are classes, women, the oppressed masses of the Third World, or a particular religious commitment.

That is not to say that emancipation in the original sense, against the weight of traditions of exploitation and oppression, is not still necessary. Millions still live under the burden of poverty and authoritarianism. But the belief that there can be a single moment of emancipatory transformation, led by the pre-ordained agent of history, can no longer carry weight in a world confronted by a multitude of emancipatory claims. The politics of emancipation, however appealing, has been no more able than the discourse of rights to provide a common set of values for coping with difference.

Rather than imagining or inventing a new emancipatory

project, we need to articulate a new imaginary which seeks to embrace both solidarity and difference. This will involve an elaboration of what Heller and Feher call 'radical tolerance', but which I prefer to call radical pluralism. In their book, the *Postmodern Political Condition*, they argue for values that are based on the two minimum universal values, of freedom and life.[39] Social systems and forms of regulation can be regarded as just insofar as they share common institutions, maximise the opportunities for communication and discourse, and are controlled by the conditional value of equality: 'equal freedom' and 'equal life chances' for all.

In a pluralistic cultural universe, there cannot be a 'good life': there are 'good lives':

> Different ways of life can be good, and can be equally good. Yet a lifestyle good for one person may not be good for another person. The authentic plurality of ways of life is the condition under which the life of each and every person can be good.[40]

It follows that the radically different life goals and patterns of life of different people should be beyond formal regulation to the extent that they are based on the conditions of equal freedom and equal life chances. Though clearly rooted in classical liberal defences of toleration, there are several ways in which this argument goes beyond them, and hence justifies the emphasis on *radical* pluralism.

Classicly, toleration implies disapproval or dislike. We do not tolerate things we like or endorse. The oldest defence of toleration derives from the religious conflicts of the seventeenth century, and is essentially a pragmatic adaptation to the murderous consequences of pursuing the truth at all costs. The concept of toleration expounded by Mill in the nineteenth century is more absolute, based on a concept of respect for the individual:

> The only freedom which deserves the name, is that of pursuing our own good in our own way, so long as we do not attempt to deprive others of theirs, or impede their efforts to obtain it.[41]

Both assume the diversity of opinions and of ways of life, the first with perhaps *realpolitik* reluctance, the second with a principled embrace of the diversity of human ends, which is explicit in Mill. Neither, however, speak of the positive promotion of diversity as a good in itself.[42]

In practical terms the results were seen in the classic debates in England in the 1960s, in the wake of the Wolfenden Report on prostitution and male homosexuality. Legal conservatives (represented by Lord Devlin) argued that a shared morality binds society together. The law, therefore, must enforce what the majority prefer. If they abhor homosexuality, then homsexuality must be criminalised (though in fact Devlin himself, as a member of the House of Lords, subsequently voted for law reform). Against this, Hart argued, from the liberal, and Wolfenden, position, that the law must balance the harm done by an action against the harm done by illegalising it: the infringement of personal liberty, the invasion of privacy, brought the law into contempt.[43]

The latter position triumphed in the sexual reform legislation of the 1960s, and continued to shape reform proposals into the 1980s (for example, over embryo research). The problem was that it satisfied neither a resurgent moral absolutism, nor the new social movements, who saw in the language of tolerance simply a confirmation of their secondary and marginal status. Only those in a position of power can tolerate the deviant minorities. It was noticeable that the reforming legislation in the 1960s did not positively embrace the value of what were previously crimes – homosexuality and abortion especially. They were simply removed from the scope of the law in certain limited circumstances.

Radical toleration attempts to go beyond these limits. Another legal peer, Lord Scarman, has put it in this way:

> I myself think that on legal, moral, cultural and aesthetic grounds a plural society is an immensely exciting opportunity for expanding human horizons, but this has got to be done consistently with democracy and consistently with the cherishing of the human rights of

those who are in a minority and of those whom perhaps
some of us dislike.[44]

Several key principles are contained in such a statement.
First, there is an assumption of the need positively to
support and encourage diversity in the interests of human
development as a whole. Secondly, there are a cluster of
values (democracy, affirmation of rights, protection of
minorities) which act as guarantees of moral pluralism.
This is more than a traditional liberal toleration, which
simply says if you do it your way, I don't mind. It involves
recognition, that other people's ways of life are our concern,
even if we do not live them ourselves. It suggests a
common concern with protecting and enhancing the lives
of others, without violating the other's negative freedom,
the freedom from interference.[45] It also means one should
be free to choose between different values, different
identities and communities.

Conclusion

The elaboration of radical pluralism into a coherent
political perspective lies beyond the scope of this paper.
What I have sought to do is rather more basic: to argue
that it is possible to develop a value system which embraces
certain principles, and by implication strategies and
policies, which accept both diversity and a wider sense of
human solidarity, without recourse to any foundationalist
arguments. The values I have explicitly espoused do, of
course, have a history. They can be traced through a
number of traditions: of humanist thought, radical and
socialist debates, the continuing unfolding of the
democratic revolution through the various spheres of
social life. They are not justified by that history, or because
of those traditions, however. They can only be argued for
in terms of certain desirable ends that they might achieve:
the enhancement of life-chances, and the maximisation of
human freedom.

Radical humanism offers not a single goal to be achieved
through a moment or process of transendence but rather a

perspective on multiple goals. There is no privileged social agent or agents to attain the ends; merely the multiplicity of local struggles against the burdens of history and the various forms of domination and subordination. Contingency, not determinism, underlies our complex present.

The openness this suggests, however, is no cause for pessimism or despair. On the contrary it provides many 'resources for hope'.[46] The navigational hazards of our postmodern journeys may sometimes appear overwhelming, but there are values aplenty to help us negotiate them successfully.

Notes

[1] John Fekete, *Life after Postmodernism, Essays on Value and Culture*, Macmillan Education, Basingstoke, 1988, p i.

[2] David McLellan, 'Introduction', in David McLellan and Sean Sayers (eds), *Socialism and Morality*, St Martin's Press, New York, 1990, p 3.

[3] Paul Feyerabend, *Farewell to Reason*, Verso, London, 1987, p 24.

[4] Michel Foucault, 'Power, Moral Values and the Intellectual: An Interview with Michel Foucault', conducted by Michael Bess, 3 November 1980, in *History of the Present*, no 4, Spring, 1988, p 13.

[5] Stuart Hall, *The Hard Road to Renewal, Thatcherism and the Crisis of the Left*, Verso, London and New York, 1989.

[6] *Ibid*, p 8.

[7] See Michael Walzer, *Interpretation and Social Criticism*, Harvard University Press, Cambridge, Mass and London, 1987.

[8] *Ibid*, p ix.

[9] *Ibid*, p 90.

[10] Ernesto Laclau, *New Reflections on the Revolution of Our Time*, Verso, London, 1989, p xiv.

[11] Hans Magnus Enzensberger, 'Enzensberger's Europe', interview by Martin Chalmers and Robert Lumley, *New Left Review*, No 178, 1989, p 102.

[12] Anthony Giddens, *Modernity and Self-Identity, Self and Society in the Later Modern Age*, Polity Press, Cambridge, 1991.

[13] Alberto Melucci, *Nomads of the Present, Social Movements and Individual Needs in Contemporary Society*, John Keane and Paul Mier (eds), Radius, London, 1989.

[14] John Stuart Mill, 'On Liberty, in *Three Essays: On Liberty, Representative Government, The Subjection of Women*, Oxford University Press, Oxford and New York 1976.

[15] Laclau, *op cit*, p 125.

[16] Walzer, *op cit*, p 32.

[17] Zygmunt Bauman, *Legislators and Interpreters: On modernity, postmodernity and intellectuals*, Polity Press, Cambridge 1989, p 143.

[18] Giddens, *op cit*, p 14.

[19] Quoted in Paul Spiker, *Principles of Social Welfare, An Introduction to thinking about the Welfare State*, Routledge, London and New York, 1988, p 10.

[20] Nancy L. Rosenblum, *Another Liberalism: Romanticism and the Reconstruction of Liberal Thought*, Harvard University Press, Cambridge, Mass and London, p 160.

[21] Alasdair MacIntyre, *Whose Justice? Which Rationality?*, University of Notre Dame Press, Notre Dame, Indiana, 1988.

[22] Quoted in David Marquand, *The Unprincipled Society, New Demands and Old Politics*, Fontana Press, London, 1988, p 220.

[23] Raymond Williams, *Culture and Society 1780-1950*, Penguin, Harmondsworth, 1962.

[24] Michael J. Sandel, *Liberalism and the Limits of Justice*, Cambridge University Press, Cambridge, 1982, p 150.

[25] Bauman, *op cit*, p 146.

[26] Anthony P. Cohen, *The Symbolic Construction of Community*, Ellis Horwood and Tavistock Publications, Chichester and London, 1985.

[27] Benedict Anderson, *Imagined Communities, Reflections on the Origin and Rise of Nationalism*, Verso, London, 1982.

[28] Laclau, *op cit*, p 245.

[29] Paul Gilroy, *'There Ain't no Black in the Union Jack': The Cultural Politics of Race and Nation*, Hutchinson, London, 1987, p 56.

[30] Kobena Mercer, 'Welcome to the Jungle: Identity and Diversity in Postmodern Politics', in Jonathan Rutherford (ed), *Identity: Community, Culture, Difference*, Lawrence and Wishart, London, 1990, p 46.

[31] Pratibha Parma, 'Black Feminism: the Politics of Articulation', in Rutherford (ed), *op cit*.

[32] Gilroy, *op cit*, p 245.

[33] Sandel, *op cit*, p 146.

[34] Stuart Hall, 'Cultural Diaspora and Identity', in Rutherford (ed), *op cit*, p 235.

[35] A.J.M. Milne, *Human Rights and Human Diversity, An Essay in the Philosophy of Human Rights*, Macmillan, London, 1986.

[36] Walzer, *op cit*, p 24.

[37] Agnes Heller, *Beyond Justice*, Basil Blackwell; Oxford 1987, p 220.

[38] See Laclau, *op cit*.

[39] Agnes Heller and Ferenc Feher, *The Postmodern Political Condition*, Polity Press, Cambridge, 1988.

[40] *Ibid*, p 323.

[41] John Stuart Mill, *op cit*, p 18.

[42] Compare Susan Mendus (ed), *Justifying Toleration: Conceptual and Historical Perspectives*, Cambridge University Press, Cambridge and New York, 1988.

[43] Mary Warnock, 'The Limits of Toleration', in Susan Mendus and David Edwards (eds), *On Toleration*, Clarendon Press, Oxford, 1987.

[44] Leslie Scarman, 'Toleration and the Law', in Mendus and Edwards (eds), *op cit*, p 62.

[45] Heller and Feher, *op cit*, p 83.
[46] Compare Raymond Williams, *Resources of Hope*, Verso, London, 1989.